Eugene O'Neill infused twentieth-century American theater with an intensity and distinction that have been its standard ever since. A winner of the 1936 Nobel prize for literature, O'Neill created such versatile works as *Beyond the Horizon* (1920), *Anna Christie* (1920), *Strange Interlude* (1928), and *The Iceman Cometh* (1939). O'Neill withheld his masterpiece, *Long Day's Journey into Night* (1941), from production during his lifetime because its troubled characters and their destructive relationships bore painful resemblance to his own family. Despite the play's overtly autobiographical elements, O'Neill's talent for language, pacing, and characterization brilliantly conveyed its universal themes. First produced in 1954, the play won O'Neill his fourth Pulitzer prize and became a landmark of American theater. In this play, as in others, O'Neill's innovative use of dramatic techniques and settings established simplicity of design as an elegant mode of theatrical presentation.

In Michael Hinden's *Long Day's Journey into Night: Native Eloquence* the author demonstrates O'Neill's twofold contribution to the arts, viewing his technical innovation and his artistic vision as the qualities that define his genius. The study provides close analysis of O'Neill's characters and language, proposing that the play's true protagonist is the family as a whole rather than any individual member. Hinden examines how the playwright's vision, comprised of a delicate balance of guilt, innocence, and pity, redefined the modern tragedy, and he presents his thesis that this play's theme is the rhythm of life itself.

Long Day's Journey into Night

Native Eloquence

Twayne's Masterwork Studies

Robert Lecker, General Editor

LONG DAY'S JOURNEY INTO NIGHT

Native Eloquence

Michael Hinden

Twayne Publishers • Boston
A Division of G.K. Hall & Co.

Long Day's Journey into Night: Native Eloquence
Michael Hinden

Twayne's Masterwork Studies No. 49

Copyright 1990 by G.K. Hall & Co.
All rights reserved.
Published by Twayne Publishers
A division of G.K. Hall & Co.
70 Lincoln Street, Boston, Massachusetts 02111

Copyediting supervised by Barbara Sutton
Book production by Gabrielle B. McDonald
Typeset in 10/14 Sabon with ITC Garamond Light display typeface
by Huron Valley Graphics, Inc., Ann Arbor, Michigan 48108

Printed on permanent/durable acid-free paper
and bound in the United States of America

Library of Congress Cataloging-in-Publication Data

Hinden, Michael.
    Long day's journey into night : native eloquence / Michael Hinden.
        p.   cm. — (Twayne's masterwork studies ; no. 49)
    Includes bibliographical references.
        1. O'Neill, Eugene, 1888–1953. Long day's journey into night.
    I. Title.   II. Series.
    PS3529.N5L636   1990
    812'.52—dc20   89-48095
                                                                            CIP

0-8057-7995-7 (alk. paper) 10 9 8 7 6 5 4 3 2 1
0-8057-8044-0 (pbk. alk. paper) 10 9 8 7 6 5 4 3 2 1
First published 1990

For my parents, Sam Hinden and Ada Trachtenberg Hinden,
who gave me a great gift: their example of happiness.

Contents

Note on the References and Acknowledgments

Quotations from *Long Day's Journey into Night* refer to the commonly available paperback edition (New Haven: Yale University Press, 1956; rpt., 1979) and are used with the permission of Yale University Press. Page numbers are included parenthetically in the citations.

I wish to thank the National Endowment for the Humanities for the award of a Travel to Collections Grant that enabled me to study O'Neill's unpublished manuscript materials at Yale University, and Patricia Willis, curator of the Collection of American Literature, Beinecke Rare Book and Manuscript Library, Yale University, for permission to quote from those materials.

The photographs that appear in this volume also are provided through the courtesy of the Collection of American Literature, Beinecke Rare Book and Manuscript Library, Yale University, and are used with permission.

Eugene O'Neill in his study at Tao House c. 1939–41, when he was working on *Long Day's Journey into Night*. Photograph courtesy of the Collection of American Literature, Beinecke Rare Book and Manuscript Library, Yale University.

Chronology: Eugene O'Neill's Life and Works

1888	Eugene Gladstone O'Neill, third son of Mary Ellen Quinlan O'Neill and James O'Neill, the actor, born 16 October in a hotel in the New York theater district.
1888–1895	Spends earliest years with his parents on theatrical road tours. Summers are spent at the family cottage on the bank of the Thames River near the entrance to the harbor at New London, Connecticut.
1895–1906	Attends a succession of religious boarding schools.
1906–1907	Enters Princeton University but is suspended in April after a drunken prank; never returns.
1908	Lives in New York, working in a mail-order house; becomes an avid devotee of the writings of Friedrich Nietzsche, the German philosopher.
1909	Marries Kathleen Jenkins on 2 October. Two weeks later, he deserts her and leaves on a gold prospecting trip to Honduras. Eugene O'Neill, Jr., born 5 May 1910.
1910–1911	Seeks adventure as an able-bodied seaman; works on sailing vessels, liners, and tramp steamers; visits ports in Africa and South America.
1912	Returns to New York and lives in a waterfront dive known as Jimmy the Priest's. Agrees to divorce Kathleen Jenkins. In January attempts suicide by taking an overdose of veronal; friends save him. Joins his father's touring company and returns with parents and brother to New London at the end of the season. Divorce finalized in October. Enters Gaylord Farm Sanatorium for treatment of tuberculosis on Christmas Eve. Discharged 3 June 1913. A watershed year: background for *Long Day's Journey into Night*.
1913–1914	Period of convalescence; determines to become "an artist or nothing." Publishes *Thirst and Other One Act Plays* in August 1914.

1914–1915   Attends Professor George Pierce Baker's playwriting course at Harvard.

1915–1916   Lives in Greenwich Village in New York, writing plays on a small allowance from his father. Spends summer in Provincetown, Massachusetts, where on 28 July 1916 his first produced play, *Bound East For Cardiff,* is mounted by the Provincetown Players.

1917–1919   First productions in New York: *The Long Voyage Home, Ile, In the Zone, The Moon of the Carribbees,* and other one-acts. Marries Agnes Boulton, a writer, on 12 April 1918. A son, Shane, born 30 October 1919.

1920   *Beyond the Horizon* produced in New York; wins Pulitzer Prize. Two additional productions: *The Emperor Jones* and *Diff'rent.* Father, James O'Neill, dies 10 August of cancer.

1921–1922   *Anna Christie* wins a second Pulitzer Prize in 1921. Additional productions: *The Hairy Ape, The Straw, The First Man.* Mother, Ella Quinlan O'Neill, dies in California of a stroke 28 February 1922.

1923   Brother, James O'Neill, Jr., dies 8 November from chronic alcoholism at age forty-five.

1924–1928   Period of O'Neill's rise to prominence. Building on the success of *The Emperor Jones* and *The Hairy Ape,* he dominates the American stage with celebrated expressionistic and experimental works: *All God's Chillun Got Wings* (1924), *Desire under the Elms* (1924), *The Fountain* (1925), *The Great God Brown* (1926), *Marco Millions* (1927), and *Lazarus Laughed* (1928). *Strange Interlude* (1928) wins him a third Pulitzer Prize. A daughter, Oona, born 13 May 1925.

1929   *Dynamo* opens to negative reviews. Divorces Agnes Boulton on 2 July and marries actress Carlotta Monterey on 22 July; lives in France and works on *Mourning Becomes Electra.*

1931   Returns to New York. *Mourning Becomes Electra* opens in October to critical acclaim.

1932   Moves to Sea Island, Georgia. Works primarily on *Days without End* (about faith and unbelief) and *Ah, Wilderness!* (his only comedy).

1933   *Ah, Wilderness!* produced in New York, a popular success.

1934   *Days without End* is a bitter failure. The beginning of twelve years in which no new O'Neill plays are staged.

1936   Awarded the Nobel Prize for literature.

Chronology

1934–1938   Works on a projected, but uncompleted, cycle of eleven plays about American history, *A Tale of Possessors Self-Dispossessed.* Builds Tao House, an Oriental-style estate in the hills near San Francisco; moves there in 1937. Beginning of decline of health and reputation.

1939–1943   At Tao House works in isolation and completes his last plays: *The Iceman Cometh* (1939), *Long Day's Journey into Night* (1941), *Hughie* (1941), *A Touch of the Poet* (1942), and *A Moon for the Misbegotten* (1943). Develops a severe tremor, which gradually ends his writing career.

1945   Returns to New York in broken health.

1946   *The Iceman Cometh* opens to mixed reviews (revived successfully in 1956 after his death).

1947   *A Moon for the Misbegotten,* the last play produced during his lifetime, opens in Columbus, Ohio, but closes before its scheduled arrival in New York (a 1973 revival draws rave reviews).

1950   Suicide of Eugene O'Neill, Jr.

1951–1952   Moves to Boston, then Marblehead, Massachusetts. Stormy quarrels with Carlotta, followed by reconciliations and periods of hospitalization for them both. Realizing he will not live to complete the eleven-play cycle, he destroys his unfinished plays. Returns to Boston, living his last two years as an invalid at the Hotel Shelton.

1953   Dies 27 November of pneumonia. His last words: "Born in a hotel room—and God damn it—died in a hotel room!"

1956   World premiere of *Long Day's Journey into Night* at the Royal Dramatic Theatre in Stockholm on 10 February. Opens on Broadway 7 November. The play wins for O'Neill his fourth Pulitzer Prize (awarded posthumously in 1957). Beginning of the O'Neill "revival."

1957–1962   American productions of *A Touch of the Poet* (1957), *Hughie* (1958), *More Stately Mansions* (1962) draw mixed reviews.

1971   Monte Cristo Cottage, O'Neill's boyhood home in New London and the setting for *Long Day's Journey into Night,* registered as a National Landmark; opens to visitors in 1978.

1976   Tao House, his home in Danville, California, where *Long Day's Journey into Night* was written, declared a National Historic Site; opens to visitors in 1985.

1980   Publication of *Poems: 1912–1944.*

1988   International celebrations and numerous productions mark the centennial of his birth.

HISTORICAL CONTEXT

1

We are the greatest example of 'For what shall it profit a man, if he shall gain the whole world, and lose his own soul?'
—*Eugene O'Neill, 1947 interview*

Eugene O'Neill belongs to American literature as well as to the theater. Like his predecessors Hawthorne, Melville, Whitman, Poe, and Emerson, he saw himself as a prophet whose task was to challenge the assumptions of his fellow citizens. O'Neill's reading of European authors and his fascination with Oriental philosophy sometimes led him on exotic intellectual adventures, but he always returned to the question of the American character and its potential for corruption. In *Long Day's Journey into Night* Mary complains that "one day long ago I found I could no longer call my soul my own" (93). At home O'Neill had *two* parents who could no longer "call their souls their own": a mother who had turned her back on life and a father who had bartered his artistic integrity for monetary success. As he grew to adulthood and began to assimilate the cultural attitudes around him, O'Neill became convinced that his family's misfortunes were symbolic of the country's misplaced values.

O'Neill developed these views in marked contrast to the mood of the nation as a whole. In the years preceding World War I, the temper of the times was expansionist and relentlessly optimistic. By then the bitter aftertaste of the Civil War had faded, and a period of stable industrial growth, fueled by cheap immigrant labor and impressive new mechanical inventions, drove the economy forward. A revolution in transportation had occurred. Sailing ships gave way to steam, horse-drawn carriages to automobiles. Homes became more comfortable through the addition of electricity, which at first was a luxury item but soon became commonplace. (To homeowners of James Tyrone's era, the repeated cry in the play of "Turn out the lights!" would not have sounded as parsimonious as it does to today's audiences.) Certainly there were stirrings of unrest during the period. Attempts to organize labor provoked bloody clashes in the 1890s, and the burgeoning women's suffrage movement disturbed conventional notions as to the role of women in society and the home; in 1888, the year of O'Neill's birth, Susan B. Anthony organized a congress in Washington, D.C., on women's rights. But the possibility of dramatic economic advancement and the assurance of stable social values were, for most white, middle-class Americans, the order of the day.

Progress was a national byword; so was daring. Americans responded vicariously to highly colored accounts of successful risk-taking. Romantic exploits provided the favorite subject matter for the stage, an apt example being James O'Neill's starring vehicle, *The Count of Monte Cristo*. Newspapers and magazines mythologized contemporary feats of exploration. The famous of the day were adventurers, showmen, and those fabled robber barons who amassed unheard-of fortunes, such as John D. Rockefeller in oil, J. P. Morgan in railroads, and Andrew Carnegie in steel. A small group of individuals owned 50 percent of the nation's wealth; they were simultaneously damned and admired. It was obvious that money was to be made in America, and many thought that if the price exacted were ethical compromise, perhaps it should be paid.

In the self-importance of the business titans O'Neill saw an arrogance that reminded him of the egotistical monarchs of the classical stage. He found support for his opinions in his reading, but he needed little prompting to galvanize his views. His father's example was sufficient. A miserably poor Irish immigrant, James O'Neill had worked his way to stardom in the theater after buying the rights to the work he referred to ever after as "that God-damned play." *The Count of Monte Cristo* was a melodramatic potboiler that dulled James's talent "through years of easy repetition" (150) and dashed his hope for fame as a serious actor. To make matters worse, he often frittered away the annual profits from his road tours in land speculation schemes that mostly failed. In *Long Day's Journey into Night* O'Neill generalizes his father's case as an American tragedy. One of the play's unforgettable moments occurs in act 4, when James Tyrone stands with upraised arms, clicking out the light bulbs in the chandelier, muttering, "What the hell was it I wanted to buy, I wonder, that was worth—Well, no matter. It's a late day for regrets" (150). For O'Neill this powerful visual image held a special irony. It recalled the famous theatrical poster of his father posing as the Count of Monte Cristo, newly escaped from prison, standing on a rocky crag that jutted from the sea and exalting with upraised arms, "The world is mine!"

Although he questioned the American ethic of success, O'Neill was not in the main a political writer. In *Long Day's Journey into Night* the world outside the Tyrone cottage slowly recedes into the distance as fog and darkness descend, and by night the family is hermetically sealed off from politics, time, and even history. The play takes place in 1912, an eventful year, but it contains no specific references to contemporary happenings. Textile workers struck in Massachusetts, the Titanic sank, Woodrow Wilson was elected President, Lenin rose to prominence in Russia, war broke out in the Balkans, Scott reached the South Pole, and cosmic rays were discovered. None of these events penetrates the fog of alcohol and morphine as the Tyrones turn ever inward, locked in their private anguish.

What mattered to O'Neill as an artist was his own experience, and in order to dramatize complex emotions, he needed to create a theater that would function as a vehicle for personal expression, not as a platform for general ideas. In his search for form he managed to reinvent American drama. Before O'Neill, the American theater had not produced a single work of undisputed literary merit, although the nineteenth-century stage was bustling with energy. Plays by notable writers and producers such as Dion Boucicault, James A. Hearn, and David Belasco showed verve and aimed for realistic effects, but few of these were intended to last as works of art. Today these plays seem marred by melodramatic situations, stilted diction, formulaic plots, stock characters, simplistic endings, or genteel restraint.

O'Neill swept the old away. Not only was his work ambitious in scale and subject matter, it also was innovative in technique. O'Neill invented a new grammar of stage presentation that mixed realistic and experimental means. He employed a variety of devices, including masks, mechanical sounds, mime, music, elaborate stage directions, brilliant visual images, and a fresh mixture of language that had not been heard before on stage: slang, colloquial English, various dialects, lyrical passages, choric voices, thought-asides, and stream-of-consciousness monologues. He imbued a variety of characters with tragic dignity and somehow made even the most inarticulate of them speak to the yearning and self-doubt that worried American audiences.

Contemplating O'Neill's revolutionary impact on the theater, the Irish dramatist Sean O'Casey wrote: "Before, the Theater had been the place of third-class jugglers and thimble-riggers, and it wasn't til O'Neill came (like Christ in the Temple) with the whip of his plays and drove those traffickers out, that Comedy and Tragedy took their places before the Theater's highest altar."[1] It happened that James O'Neill was in the audience on opening night of *Beyond the Horizon,* the first of O'Neill's full-length plays to be produced in New York. The old actor had once shared the stage with Edwin Booth, the brother of Lincoln's assassin, and now, nearly fifty years later, his son was succeeding him in a theatrical career. James was puzzled by what he saw; he wondered aloud whether his son were trying to send the audience home to commit suicide.[2] But assuredly he was proud. Whatever passed between father and son on that occasion, an era passed on the American stage.

4

THE IMPORTANCE OF
THE WORK

2

Stammering is the native eloquence of us fog people.
——Edmund, *Long Day's Journey into Night,* act 4

Although O'Neill had been a successful playwright since the 1920s, his finest work came late, built on a lifetime's accumulation of stage experience and wisdom. "Hereafter I write plays primarily as literature to be read—and the more simply they read, the better they will act, no matter what the technique."[3] Austerity, simplicity, and biting honesty are the attributes of the best of his late plays: *The Iceman Cometh, Long Day's Journey into Night,* and *A Moon For the Misbegotten.* In these works thematic statement is absorbed entirely by the dramatic action rather than imposed upon the characters by design, which may have been a fault in some of O'Neill's earlier plays. Characters are delineated with greater subtlety. Language is unstrained. Retrospection is the mood, guilt and forgiveness are at the core. The most moving of these is *Long Day's Journey into Night;* it is, by common critical assent, our best American play.

What specific attributes entitle us to term the play a masterwork? The simplicity of the play's dramatic form; the complexity of its four major characters and the progressive unfolding of their psychological richness; the directness of their presentation without gimmickry or sentimentality; the absorbing emotional rhythm of their interactions; the intensity of their quest for meaning; the natural yet expressive quality of their dialogue; their insights concerning guilt, vulnerability, and the need for family connection—these are among the qualities that have gained for the play its status as a world classic. *Long Day's Journey into Night* simultaneously marks the pinnacle of O'Neill's career and the coming of age of American drama.

If the play is O'Neill's autobiography, its vision of family life is harrowing. The Tyrones attack one another without quarter. Sometimes only exhaustion intervenes to call a truce. But in equal measure they are able to share their most intimate dreams. What family would ever want to be that close, or would settle for anything less? In this respect the Tyrones speak to our deepest fears and desires. Perhaps one reason for the play's enormous emotional appeal is the undeniable truth that it continually asserts: we all demand to be loved unconditionally by our families.

Of course the theme of family is international, but it seems to have a particular claim upon Americans. In the absence of a rigid social structure organized by tradition, class, or overriding ethnic alliances, American culture depends heavily on the family unit to frame identity. Threats to the integrity of the family have provided the subject for the most celebrated plays in the American repertory: *Awake and Sing* by Clifford Odets, *The Glass Menagerie* by Tennessee Williams, *Death of a Salesman* by Arthur Miller, *The Little Foxes* by Lillian Hellman, *Our Town* by Thornton Wilder, *A Raisin in the Sun* by Lorraine Hansberry, *Who's Afraid of Virginia Woolf?* by Edward Albee, *I Never Sang for My Father* by Robert Anderson, *Buried Child* by Sam Shepard, and *Fences* by August Wilson, to name but a few. Towering over them all is *Long Day's Journey into Night*, which sets the standard for an American genre.

Like most great works of literature, *Long Day's Journey into Night* also reaches beyond its immediate subject. O'Neill's play is dedicated not only to the life of the American family, but (in Edmund

Tyrone's phrase) "to the life of Man, to Life itself!" (153). As its title suggests, the play compresses into the space of a few hours the human experience of life's inexorable passage toward closure. Youthful hope, first failure, the turmoil of middle age, and the faded dreams of the old all pass before us in a unified flow.

O'Neill's ability to evoke the rhythm of lived experience stems from his genius for pacing and his masterful shaping of the realistic idiom. Dramatic language was not his greatest gift, but in this play at last O'Neill was able to turn the simplest conversational prose into a medium of emotional conviction. Consider the final sentences of Mary's beautiful monologue on the brevity of life: "That was in the winter of senior year. Then in the spring something happened to me. Yes, I remember. I fell in love with James Tyrone and was so happy for a time" (176). The speech captures the mood of those memorable lines from *The Tempest* quoted earlier by James and successfully recasts them into modern idiom: "We are such stuff as dreams are made on, / and our little life is rounded with a sleep" (131). Mary's reflection is homely and specific, Prospero's is general and grand; but that the two speeches inhabit the same play without gross disproportion is testimony to O'Neill's linguistic triumph. One of the most significant attributes of *Long Day's Journey into Night* is its expressive realism, the achievement of what Edmund in the fourth act of the play aptly describes as "native eloquence."

COMPOSITION AND CRITICAL RECEPTION

3

[I] like this play better than any I have ever written.

—O'Neill, *Work Diary*

COMPOSITION

At Tao House, O'Neill's estate in the hills of the San Ramon Valley near Danville, California, fog sometimes rolls in from the foot of Mount Diablo. Looking up from his desk and gazing out the east window of a study lined with books and models of sailing ships, O'Neill was carried back to his boyhood home a continent away. On sunny mornings he could adjust the blinds or else take his writing pad to another desk to avoid the glare, but on gloomy mornings he could look out at the valley and write as he watched the fog. It was in this room in the summer of 1939 that O'Neill began working on *Long Day's Journey into Night*.

In Europe the Second World War was threatening. For the past decade O'Neill's reputation had been in eclipse. His health was no longer robust, and the cycle of plays on American history that he had undertaken was defeating him. His last New York production (*Days without End* in 1934) had been a failure. Depressed and withdrawn, O'Neill turned inward, no longer writing for the public but for himself. Under these conditions he began working on "a play of old sorrow," as he called it, probing his family's history. Later his wife confided to an interviewer: "When he started *Long Day's Journey*, it was a most strange experience to watch that man being tortured every day by his own writing. He would come out of his study at the end of a day gaunt and sometimes weeping. His eyes would be all red and he looked ten years older than when he went in in the morning. I think he felt freer when he got it out of his system. It was his way of making peace with his family—and himself."[4]

O'Neill kept a detailed work diary, and as a result, it is possible to trace the progress of the play's composition.[5] During the early stages of the play's development, O'Neill was working on several projects at once. The first mention of *Long Day's Journey* occurs on 6 June 1939, when "fed up and stale" on the American history cycle after four-and-a-half years "of not thinking of any other work" (5 June comment), O'Neill decides to sketch the outlines for two plays that "appeal most." One is a "N[ew]. L[ondon]. family" play; the other would become *The Iceman Cometh*. Yet during that month, he spent four days on *The Calms of Capricorn* (an unfinished cycle play), seventeen days on the outline for *Iceman*, and only six days on what he was then calling "The Long Day's Journey." On 3 July he finished the outline for *Long Day's Journey* and noted the weather as "cold fog." He turned next to *The Iceman Cometh*, concentrating on that play throughout September, October, and November, and completing it in December. On 3 January 1940, he did some final "trimming" of *The Iceman Cometh;* on the fourth he made notes for a "comedy with the tentative title 'The Visit of Malatesta' " (uncompleted); on the fifth, he read over the outline for "The Long Day's Journey" and urged himself to "do this soon"; then on the sixth, he was mired again in the history cycle and unable to proceed. However, by February, he was thinking again of his "New London" play. He adopted the title "Long Day's Journey into Night" on the twenty-second.

By March 1940 O'Neill was ready to put aside his faltering comedy and devote himself to the play that mattered most. He broke off work on "The Visit of Malatesta," ending the manuscript with two cryptic lines: "To the Day! / To the Night!"[6] The reference may have been a simultaneous farewell to the comic play, which he felt himself temperamentally unsuited to write, and an embrace of the tragic drama, to which he now turned. Throughout April, May, and June of 1940, O'Neill worked steadily on *Long Day's Journey into Night*, pausing only to reflect on the dark news from the war in Europe. By July a first draft of act 1 was complete; by the end of August he had finished first drafts of acts 2 and 3. In September he worked on act 4, and began rewriting on the twenty-first. On 16 October 1940 he recorded that he was finished with the second draft and noted the date as his fifty-second birthday. He then returned for a short while to the American history cycle and spent the winter sketching out new ideas for several other plays, none of which came to fruition. On 17 March 1941 he picked up *Long Day's Journey* again to cut and revise. Mrs. O'Neill had typed the manuscript from her husband's crabbed handwritten copy, and on 30 March the playwright reviewed the typescript and made his final cuts. On that date the following entry appears in the *Work Diary:* "Second & I think final draft—like this play better than any I have ever written—does the most with the least—a quiet play!—and a great one, I believe."[7] O'Neill added a final touch on 1 April, expanding Tyrone's monologue in act 4 to include details of his early acting career.[8]

Because of the play's sensitive personal nature, O'Neill stipulated that *Long Day's Journey into Night* not be published or produced until at least twenty-five years after his death. According to these terms, the play could not have been released until 1978. However, O'Neill's widow, Carlotta Monterey O'Neill, decided to let the play be staged by the Swedish Royal Dramatic Theatre in 1956. Her decision caused considerable controversy. According to Mrs. O'Neill's account, her husband withdrew his prohibition in a private conversation with her shortly before he died. The reason for the original restriction, she claimed, had been the uneasiness of O'Neill's son, Eugene O'Neill, Jr., at the prospect of having family matters aired in public. After the latter's suicide in 1950, she maintained, the restriction no longer held. Moreover, she said the playwright had consigned the work to her as a "nest egg" in the event that she needed money. She added that early release of the play would be instrumental in reviving her late husband's flagging reputation.[9]

Others doubted this account. O'Neill's publisher at Random House, Saxe Commins, who was one of the playwright's oldest friends, disputed Mrs. O'Neill's intention to violate the terms of her husband's will. Through him O'Neill had deposited the play in the Random House vault, and Commins had received no further communication from the playwright contradicting his original directive.[10] In order to carry out his friend's wishes, Commins enlisted the support of Bennett Cerf, then head of Random House, and together they refused to accede to Mrs. O'Neill's request. She then withdrew the work from the Random House safe, which was her legal right as O'Neill's executrix. Cerf relinquished publication rights to the play, and Mrs. O'Neill gave it to Yale University Press, at the same time arranging for the play's world premiere in Stockholm. The dispute by now had become public and had generated much interest. Albert Einstein, Saxe Commins's neighbor in Princeton, New Jersey, dryly observed to him one day: "The lady is determined to exhume Gene's body."[11]

PRODUCTION HISTORY

The success of the play's opening abroad, followed swiftly by its publication and Broadway premiere, soon overwhelmed any questions about the propriety of its release. Mrs. O'Neill chose the Royal Dramatic Theatre of Stockholm for the premiere partly because the Swedes had mounted a successful production of *A Moon for the Misbegotten* in 1953 after its failure in the United States, and partly because the theater's director had prevailed upon Dag Hammarskjöld, then secretary general of the United Nations, to gain permission to stage the play in Stockholm. The play opened on 10 February 1956 to coincide with the American publication of the text. Swedish theater critics were lavish in their praise, judging O'Neill's work by the dimensions of Aeschylus and Shakespeare (not to mention Strindberg and Ibsen). The production turned into the greatest success in the history of the Royal Dramatic.[12] American audiences had to wait until November for the English language premiere of *Long Day's Journey into Night*. By then, word of the play's reception in Europe had preceded it, and anticipation was high.

Opening night at the Helen Hayes Theater in New York on 7 November 1956 was a memorable occasion. Under José Quintero's direction, a distinguished cast performed to wide acclaim. Fredric March, the venerable stage and screen actor, played the father, James Tyrone; Florence Eldridge triumphed as Mary, the mother; Jason Robards, Jr., made his reputation in the part of Jamie, the elder brother; Bradford Dillman played the younger brother, Edmund; and Katherine Ross was the serving girl, Cathleen. A sampling of opening-night reviews suggests the unusual degree of enthusiasm with which the play was received. Walter Kerr of the *New York Herald Tribune* found the production "a stunning theatrical experience."[13] John Chapman of the *Daily News* pronounced *Long Day's Journey* to be "O'Neill's most beautiful play . . . and . . . one of the great dramas of any time."[14] Brooks Atkinson of the *New York Times* wrote that with the advent of *Long Day's Journey into Night,* the "American theater acquires stature and size,"[15] and Henry Hewes, in the *Saturday Review,* called the work "the most universal piece of stage realism ever turned out by an American playwright."[16] One or two critics voiced minor reservations. Robert Coleman of the *New York Mirror* thought the play repetitious,[17] and Richard Cooke of the *Wall Street Journal* was bothered by its length.[18] But the major New York critics were united in their opinion that the posthumous debut of *Long Day's Journey into Night* marked a signal event in the history of American theater.

Subsequent productions of *Long Day's Journey into Night* have confirmed its reputation. A dramatic text is destined for performance, and one of the signs of a great dramatic work is its amenability to different interpretations depending on the director and a given cast. By now *Long Day's Journey into Night* has been performed countless times, and the work's production history richly demonstrates the play's many possibilities as a stage vehicle. The off-Broadway revival of the play in 1971 is a case in point. This production was directed by Arvin Brown and featured Geraldine Fitzgerald as Mary, Robert Ryan as Tyrone, Stacy Keach as Jamie, James Naughton as Edmund, and Paddy Croft as Cathleen. Fitzgerald's performance attracted particular notice. After considerable research into the effects of morphine addiction, she played Mary Tyrone as increasingly excitable as the evening wore on, whereas other actresses had chosen to emphasize her drowsiness. Critics found this performance riveting. In 1981 Fitzgerald went on to direct a successful production of the play that featured an African-American cast, demonstrating once again the play's openness to change.

No doubt more people have seen the movie version of the play than any single stage production. Fortunately, despite extensive cutting, the 1962 black-and-white film remains faithful to the spirit of the text. Directed by Sidney Lumet, its cast includes the British actor Sir Ralph Richardson as James Tyrone, Katharine Hepburn as Mary, Jason Robards, Jr., as Jamie, Dean Stockwell as Edmund, and Jeanne Barr as Cathleen. Robards's interpretation of Jamie re-creates his electrifying stage performance; none of its original power seems diminished on the screen. Stockwell suggests an interesting approach to the relationship between the two brothers by playing Edmund as weak and easily dominated. Hepburn's Mary is surprisingly youthful, mannered, and flirtatious. Perhaps the most moving performance is given by Richardson as James Tyrone. His physical resemblance to James O'Neill is uncanny, and his projection of dignity mingled with gentle befuddlement is especially effective. One highlight of the film occurs as the camera moves in on a close-up of Richardson's face as he registers successive waves of pain as Edmund berates him for his miserly ways.

Certain concessions were made in the filming, but they are balanced by intelligent additions. Film is a medium that privileges the eye, whereas theater privileges the ear. It is not surprising that a number of speeches were cut in the film and that some new scenes were added to supplement the closed set of the stage. The opening scene in the film, for example, takes place outdoors. The Tyrones breakfast on their porch (which is mentioned in the play but never seen on stage) and then continue their dialogue ambling down the lawn toward the river. The first scene between Jamie and his father is set in a combination workshed/garage, where we actually see the secondhand automobile that James has purchased for Mary's outings. Director Lumet adds an appropriate visual detail as the characters converse. Tyrone busies himself sharpening a file while complaining about his son's aborted acting career, a cinematic allusion to his own early days in a machine shop where he made files before embarking on the stage. A moment later Tyrone catches his finger in a vise, suggesting the trap he set for himself with that big money-making play. Such details indicate Lumet's respect for the text and account for the creativity and integrity of his screen adaptation.

Two important revivals of the play present a study in contrast. The first, starring Jack Lemmon as Tyrone, Bethel Leslie as Mary, Kevin Spacey as Jamie, Peter Gallagher as Edmund, and Jodie McClintock as Cathleen, opened at the Broadhurst Theatre on 28 April 1986; it was later televised in 1988. Jonathan Miller's direction was controversial, and the production received decidedly mixed reviews. Miller instructed the cast to overlap their lines, as if to imitate the confusion that often characterizes family quarrels in everyday life. The result was a frenetic, fast-paced theatrical evening with sallies of stinging ripostes. But for many critics the performance lacked emotional density. O'Neill's deliberate pacing has a purpose in *Long Day's Journey into Night,* and Miller's disregard for the play's internal momentum was costly (he shaved an hour from the normal playing time). Critics thought that Bethel Leslie's clinical portrait of Mary's response to morphine addiction largely drained her character of appeal. By comparison, Fitzgerald's similar approach to the role in 1971 reserved for the character a degree of warmth and vulnerability. Jack Lemmon's conception of Tyrone was that of a mugging ham actor, essentially a caricature.

In contrast to the Jonathan Miller production, José Quintero's remounting of the play in the spring of 1988 as part of the O'Neill centennial was roundly satisfying. Recalling his direction of the original American production thirty years earlier, Quintero told an interviewer, "I understood the problems of the young members of the family, and I imagined, I think, the problems of the father and mother. Now, of course, I look at the play and my feelings are more with the parents. So I have viewed the play from both sides."[19] Quintero's evolving vision was underscored by the transformation of Jason Robards, Jr., from Jamie in the 1956 production to the senior Tyrone in the centennial revival. In Robards's interpretation Tyrone was as much the professional actor as he was in Lemmon's reading: convivial, attractive, attention seeking, and oratorical. But in addition, Robards projected a stoical mask thinly covering his character's deep inner suffering. The picture of the actor standing on a chair to attack the light bulbs in his chandelier and not losing a shred of nobility (or any of his lines) was especially memorable. The rest of the cast was equally strong. Frank Rich of the *Times* praised Colleen Dewhurst for her unsentimentalized and controlled performance as Mary: "She's a killer, forever twisting the knife in old family wounds."[20] Campbell Scott was an impressive Edmund, believably sick but capable of passion and anger. Jamey Sheridan made a credible Jamie, too (though the shadow of Robards's stamp on the part in both the 1956 production and the film inevitably dogged him, as Robards was there in the flesh to recall it). The 1988 Quintero revival was perhaps the most distinguished production of the play since its 1956 opening and a salutary indication of its ever renewable stage life.

RECEPTION OF THE TEXT

The publication of *Long Day's Journey into Night* in 1956 was greeted with a degree of enthusiasm equal to its stage premiere. In the years since its first reviews (the Yale paperback edition has been reprinted more than fifty times), the play has achieved unquestioned status as an American classic. No other play by O'Neill or any other American playwright has garnered as much esteem. (Rival claimants in production popularity might be Miller's *Death of a Salesman,* Williams's *A Streetcar Named Desire,* or Wilder's *Our Town,* but none of these enjoys a comparable literary reputation.) Even Robert Brustein, who dismisses most of O'Neill's earlier work as lacking in aesthetic merit, elevates *Long Day's Journey into Night* to the status of a great work of art.[21]

Among major American critics of dramatic literature, only Eric Bentley has persisted in his negative opinion of O'Neill's work. What O'Neill did in the theater, he maintains, was to take Victorian melodrama and add his own private and neurotic complexes.[22] Bentley had contended as early as 1946 that O'Neill was no thinker, stating that his plays lacked philosophical and political content.[23] No doubt this view has continued to color his assessment of the playwright's work. Many other critics have found the play challenging on intellectual grounds. The scholarly literature is alive with interesting examinations of the text's multiple dimensions.[24] Critics have discussed the play's extension of the naturalistic tradition, its philosophical stance, its application of Freudian and/or Jungian insights, its use of late nineteenth-century ideas, its symbolism, its language, its status as a modern tragedy, its treatment of human relationships, its view of relativism and/or truth, its conception of time, its sociological implications, and of course its analysis of family life. Controversy has arisen over several specific issues. Who is the central character in the play? Who chiefly is to blame for the family's woes? Are we to accept Mary's claim that none of us can help the things that life has done to us? Is the play fatalistic in that sense? Moreover, if the play is autobiographical, how accurate are the portraits that O'Neill paints of the individual members of his family, including himself?

One recent trend in O'Neill criticism is to value how the play directly anticipates contemporary concerns. Readers now are discussing Mary's plight from the perspective of feminist analysis.[25] Several critics have examined the work in terms of its portrayal of alcoholism and drug addiction.[26] One prominent O'Neill scholar suggests that the problems of the Tyrones are typical of those of Irish-American families in general and that the play is more revealing "as a cultural document" than it is as an autobiographical one.[27] These views are stimulating and add to our appreciation of the play's broader context, but in the end it may be an error to deemphasize the uniqueness of the Tyrones' situation. As Tolstoy reminds us in the opening sentence of *Anna Karenina*, "All happy families resemble one another, but each unhappy family is unhappy in its own way."[28] In approaching the play it might be prudent to bear in mind Tolstoy's caution.

a reading

CURTAIN UP: SETTING AND DRAMATIC STRUCTURE

4

It's the foghorn I hate. It won't let you alone.

—Mary, *Long Day's Journey into Night*, act 3

THE SET

Readers of *Long Day's Journey into Night* often are intrigued by the play's elaborate stage directions. These descriptions are evidence of O'Neill's desire to control every aspect of production, even though the actors and director are at liberty to contravene them. "I hardly ever go to the theater," the playwright remarked in later life, "although I read all the plays I can get. I don't go to the theater because I can always do a better production in my mind than the one on the stage."[29] This comment suggests another motive for O'Neill's extensive stage directions: they are addressed not only to the actor but also the reader, who is invited to visualize an imaginary production. In a sense O'Neill assumes the prerogative of a novelist, specifying in the most minute detail the look of a room, the objects within it, and the physical appearance of his characters. Such fidelity to detail also demonstrates

The set designed by David Hays for the 1956 Broaadway premiere of *Long Day's Journey into Night*. Photograph courtesy of the Collection of American Literature, Beinecke Rare Book and Manuscript Library, Yale University.

the particular importance that setting held for O'Neill, for he believed that place was a reflection of personality. Therefore, O'Neill's introductory paragraphs are crucial components of the play. The reader is required to visualize the space in which the characters interact.

As the curtain rises in the theater, we are shown the interior of the Tyrones' summer cottage. According to the stage directions, the set suggests a sparsely furnished, rather casual-looking living room. The hardwood floor is partly covered with a nondescript rug. The furnishings include a wicker couch with cushions, three wicker armchairs, and an oak rocker—pieces indicating a vacation home rather than a well-appointed permanent residence. A small wicker table and an oak desk along the right wall, two little bookcases, and a round table center stage complete the main items of the set. To outward appearances, the room seems pleasant enough, but as Mary complains later, everything appears to be done in the cheapest way. Before a word is spoken, the set visually presents one of Mary's grievances against her husband.

Throughout the day Mary yearns for a "place I could go to get away" (46). Not only Mary, but all the Tyrones chafe in these close quarters, and once during the day each of them flees: Tyrone visits the barroom, Jamie the brothel, Edmund his doctor and then the beach, and Mary the drugstore, where she replenishes her supply of morphine. But Mary, more than the others, feels trapped in this smallish, ramshackle house, which is flooded with deceptively cheerful sunlight at 8:30 in the morning on a day in August 1912.

Each of the key props tells us something particular about the characters. On the round table at center stage stands a green shaded reading lamp awkwardly plugged into one of the sockets in the chandelier above. The dangling electric cord speaks of Tyrone's parsimony; the light lacks a proper outlet. Later, in the fourth act, we learn that Tyrone uses this little reading lamp as a substitute for the overhead bulbs in order to reduce his electrical bills. The table on which the lamp stands functions as the centerpiece of the room. The characters place themselves around it, draw up to it, then push away. Several times during the play Mary nervously drums her fingers on the tabletop. On other occasions her hands rove over the table aimlessly toying with small objects. At one point Tyrone covers her nervously roaming hand with his own in an attempt to calm her. In acts 2, 3, and 4 the table displays a tray with a bottle of whiskey, some glasses, and a pitcher of water. These items, too, become focal points as the play develops. Jamie, Edmund, and even Mary resort to watering Tyrone's whiskey after surreptitiously depleting his bottle. In act 4 we see Tyrone sitting alone with two bottles in front of him but only one light bulb on in the room. By that point we no longer need to be told that Tyrone is drinking too much or that he is dreadfully stingy. The stage props visually reinforce what we already know.

O'Neill uses each piece of furniture in the room to maximum effect. For example, the placement of chairs on the stage makes powerful visual statements as characters turn them toward or away from one another. Several times during the play Mary half-sits on the arm of Edmund's chair rather than face him directly: "*She gets him to sit and she sits sideways on the arm of his chair, an arm around his shoulder, so he cannot meet her eyes*" (91–92). Tyrone repeats the gesture with Jamie: "*Tyrone comes to the table and sits down, turning his chair so he won't look at Jamie*" (169). Mary's final entrance recapitulates the various moments in the play when characters withdraw from one another. "*She moves like a sleepwalker, around the back of Jamie's chair, then forward toward left front, passing behind Edmund*" (174). She has been moving behind Edmund throughout the play. This time he can bear it no longer. He reaches out and grabs her arm, but she shakes him off and isolates herself by perching on the front end of the sofa facing the audience. It is from this position, with her hands folded in her lap, that she delivers the closing monologue.

One of the most unusual aspects of O'Neill's opening set description is the detailed survey that he provides of the titles in the two bookcases on stage. Later in the play the audience learns about the reading matter in Edmund's bookcase (which stands against the rear wall, facing the audience) when Tyrone gestures toward it and complains about Edmund's taste: "That damned library of yours! *He indicates the small bookcase at rear.* Voltaire! Rousseau, Schopenhauer, Nietzsche, Ibsen! Atheists, fools, and madmen!" (135). Edmund's favorites are exclusively modern and, for the most part, radical authors, whether in literature, politics, or philosophy. He also champions Dowson, Baudelaire, Swinburne, Wilde, Whitman, Poe, Rossetti, and Zola as iconoclasts. In contrast, the second bookcase, located toward the back of the left wall, contains Tyrone's library, which represents his nationalistic and more conservative tastes. Here (in addition to three sets of Shakespeare) are Victor Hugo, Charles Lever (a nineteenth-century Irish author of historical novels), Tobias Smollett, Edward Gibbon, several histories of Ireland, miscellaneous volumes of old plays, and a set of the "*World's Best Literature in fifty large volumes*" (11). O'Neill adds that the astonishing thing about these books is that they all "*have the look of having been read and reread.*" These remarks are obviously meant for the reader and not the audience, but they do serve a dramatic purpose. The catalog of titles informs us of the antagonistic philosophies of father and son, and prepares the context for a battle of the books that takes place later in the play. In this regard, one of the most prominent features of the set is a portrait of Shakespeare that hangs above the rear wall bookcase. This portrait obviously is one of Tyrone's prized possessions. Edmund's "damned library" sitting beneath it is a sassy challenge meant to provoke his father.

Doorways are crucial to a functioning stage set. There are three in the Tyrones' living room—a screen door leading out onto the porch and two good-sized double doors on the rear wall flanking Edmund's bookcase. The one at right leads into a front parlor. "*The other opens on a dark, windowless back parlor, never used except as a passage from living room to dining room* (11). There is something faintly menacing about O'Neill's description of this shadowy back parlor.[30] It leads to the dining room, but the family's passage through it becomes increasingly unhappy during the day. For example, at the opening curtain Tyrone and Mary enter gaily from the back parlor following their breakfast. Tyrone's arm is around his wife's waist, and he gives her a playful hug as they enter. However, there is a pointed change when they reappear through the same entranceway after lunch. Tyrone now is no longer close to Mary; he even avoids touching or looking at her. As the day wears on, Mary begins to "disappear" through the back parlor, and Edmund considers hiding in it to avoid confronting his mother when she comes down the stairs. The back parlor, then, seems to be an avenue of retreat toward privacy.

In contrast to the darkened back parlor, the front parlor is a site of light and sound. The telephone is located there; it rings during the play with Dr. Hardy's call regarding Edmund's condition. The hall light is placed there as well. The front parlor is the family's main transit to the outside world—and release. During act 2 Tyrone moves toward the front parlor preparing to leave the house, but Mary restrains him by clasping his arm. The doorway to the front parlor also doubles as the main passage to the staircase leading to the second floor. Mary enters from the front parlor in the second act after taking one of her injections. Her dramatic fourth-act entrance is also through this doorway, accompanied by a burst of light and music. It is in the front parlor (out of sight of the audience) that she pauses to grope out a tune on the piano before hesitating on the threshold *"like someone who has come into a room to get something but has become absent-minded on the way and forgotten what it was"* (170). In her heavily drugged state, Mary finally is removed from the prison of her surroundings. Although she enters the family living room, she could not be more distant from her sons and husband, who now seem to her objects indistinguishable from the furniture.

Although the living room is the only part of the Tyrone home that we actually see on stage, we are encouraged to imagine additional parts of the house through references and implication.[31] Apparently there is a dining room beyond the back parlor and off that a kitchen, which is the domain of Bridget, the cook. There is a cellar, where James stores his whiskey, and a porch that extends halfway around the house. (In act 4 Tyrone hides on the porch, standing outside in the damp chill to avoid meeting Jamie.) Upstairs there is a complete second floor and above that a storage attic, where Mary keeps her wedding dress in a trunk. The bathroom is on the second floor, as are four small bedrooms: one for James and Mary, one for each of the brothers, and an ominous "spare room" to which Mary retreats for her morphine injections. This extra room would have belonged to baby Eugene, had he not died. Mary haunts the second floor from the afternoon through the evening. The men continually glance upwards, worrying and reminding us of Mary's suspected activity in the spare room.

Finally, there are two rows of windows in the living room opening to the outside. According to O'Neill's directions, a series of windows along the right wall looks over the front lawn to the harbor and the avenue that runs along the waterfront. A similar series of windows in the left wall looks out on the grounds in the back of the house. The wicker couch is placed beneath these windows. During the early part of the play, characters look out through these windows and report what they see, thus expanding the imaginary horizon of the set. For example, Mary watches Jamie and Tyrone cutting the hedge and observes the Chatfields passing. As the day wears on, characters drift toward the windows not to engage the world but to avert their eyes from the scene inside. *"Jamie gets up and goes to the windows at right, glad of an excuse to turn his back*" (61). As Edmund approaches the doorway in the second act, Mary "*goes swiftly away to the windows at left and stares out with her back to the front parlor*" because she cannot face him (89). Gradually the windows of the Tyrone living room begin to darken. After lunch, although the day is still fine, no sunlight penetrates the room, and by night the fog has rolled in from the Sound, blocking off the outside "*like a white curtain*" drawn across the windows (97). Then the set, which appeared so cheerful in the morning, becomes claustrophobic, closing in oppressively on the characters.

Thus O'Neill's simple one-room set functions in several important ways. Of course it provides a venue for character interactions, but it also becomes a hiding place where characters dodge one another physically and psychologically. Exits, props, windows, and even furniture become instruments of isolation as the evening turns to night.

THE SOCIAL SETTING

There is a world outside the fog-bound cottage, and O'Neill develops interesting strategies to remind the audience of its existence. The larger social setting of the play extends beyond the stage to include a sense of time, place, and community. The unnamed town in which the Tyrones live (modeled on New London, Connecticut, as O'Neill remembered it) is conjured up in a variety of indirect ways. We know that the Tyrones live toward the outskirts of this coastal town because to reach the center they must take a trolley. Their cottage is very near the water. The foghorn on the lighthouse is close enough to sound like "a sick whale in the back yard" (17). Although we are told that the Tyrones took up residence here to be close to some of Mary's relatives, they now appear to be isolated. They are on intimate terms neither with the locals nor with the wealthier city people such as the Chatfields who arrive for the summer. Tyrone himself has a great following in the barroom and at his club, but as an actor and an Irish immigrant he cannot penetrate the Chatfields' social stratum. With these "big frogs in a small puddle" (43) he has a nodding acquaintance only. (Rather than nod to the Chatfields as they drive by, Jamie ducks down in embarrassment while he is trimming the hedge.) Tyrone knows perfectly well that he cannot keep up with the gentry. The Chatfields own a Mercedes; he keeps a secondhand Packard. He frets that he will be taken for one of the rich summer residents by the local merchants and professional men, so he "dresses down" and pleads empty pockets. As a result, Mary complains that she is treated as a social outcast. The neighbors in turn regard her as peculiar and withdrawn and discourage their daughters from socializing with her sons.

The spectrum of town society and the Tyrones' ambivalent niche in it are suggested through Edmund's humorous account of the Shaughnessy-Harker dispute. Tyrone's reactions reveal his uncomfortable relationship with both his tenant farmer, Shaughnessy, a fellow Irishman who clearly is beneath him on the social scale, and his Yankee neighbor Harker, "the Standard Oil millionaire." Shaughnessy has a glorious romp accusing Harker of "enticing" his pigs into Harker's ice pond, where they have been wallowing in pleasure (and spoiling the water for next year's ice). At first Tyrone worries what Harker will think of him in his capacity as Shaughnessy's landlord. He scowls and calls the farmer "a wily Shanty Mick" (22). But soon Tyrone's own Irish pride wins out, and he joins in the laughter. Jamie interrupts the festivity with a trenchant remark: "I'll bet the next time you see Harker at the Club and give him the old respectful bow, he won't see you" (23). Jamie knows his father's manner as well as the town's unspoken social rules. Tyrone no doubt will nod to Harker only to be repaid with a snub.

Through such anecdotes O'Neill limns a subtle portrait of the town, sketching a cross section of society. From time to time O'Neill suggests the existence of secondary characters who never appear in the flesh. Besides the Chatfields, Harker, and Shaughnessy, the population includes Bridget the cook, McGuire the real estate agent, a snooty unnamed druggist, Smythe the chauffeur, Dr. Hardy, a certain Captain Turner who stops for conversation at the hedge, as well as Mamie Burns and Fat Violet, who are particular acquaintances of Jamie. Taken together, these townspeople, rich and poor, respectable and disreputable, create the illusion of a colorful community that exists beyond the confines of the summer cottage and its four bickering inhabitants.

THE FOG

If O'Neill establishes the play's social setting through its secondary characters, he establishes its natural setting through allusions to the fog. The Tyrones' cottage takes its charm from its proximity to the sea, but it also absorbs moodiness from the menacing fog that rolls off the water to gradually envelop it. During the day each of the characters mentions the fog, but its effect upon Mary and Edmund is profound. O'Neill regarded the fog as a crucial symbolic element in the play; his original manuscript notes include a memorandum on "weather progression" that links the fog to Mary's drug addiction. As O'Neill suggests in his outline, after the mother takes morphine, "she likes the fog, foghorn—finally becomes unconscious of it—while it drives [the] rest of them crazy."[32]

At the beginning of the play the foghorn gives Mary an excuse to sleep in the spare room. It keeps Edmund awake, too. The fog becomes for him a marker of time as he strains his ears, "listening for the slightest sound, hearing the fog drip from the eaves like the uneven tick of a rundown, crazy clock" (152). The foghorn moans "like a banshee," but Mary hardly can hear it by act 3 because she *has hidden deeper within herself and found refuge and release in a dream*" (97). The fog "hides you from the world and the world from you. . . . No one can find or touch you any more" (98). She fears the foghorn, which pierces the fog, calling her back to reality. As the drug takes effect, Mary becomes increasingly attuned to the fog. Tyrone, in a barbed remark, acknowledges the connection:

TYRONE: We're in for another night of fog, I'm afraid.

MARY: Oh, well, I won't mind it tonight.

TYRONE: No, I don't imagine you will, Mary. (82)

The moan of the foghorn does call Mary back at the end of act 3, snapping her out of her reverie. However, this moment of lucidity is brief. By the fourth act, Mary is lost again in the fog. As Edmund puts it: "The hardest thing to take is the blank wall she builds around her. Or it's more like a bank of fog in which she hides and loses herself" (139).

Throughout the third act Mary does evince ambivalent feelings toward the fog, which suggests her inner struggle against the drugged oblivion that beckons her. To Cathleen, she confides: "It wasn't the fog I minded, Cathleen. I really love fog" (98); but not long after, when the men return, she complains of the foggy evening that depresses her and pleads for their company (112). Later she asks Edmund, "Why is it fog makes everything sound so sad and lost, I wonder?" (121). Yet in spite of her struggle, the attraction of the fog is too powerful for Mary, and at the end of the act she steals away upstairs to lose herself for the remainder of the night in the oblivion of morphine.

As Mary slips away from them, the men begin to drink more heavily, using alcohol to induce their own mental fog. By the fourth act Jamie is a staggering drunk. Edmund also has had too much to drink, although like his father he carries it well. Tyrone himself has consumed a quantity of liquor; his eyes *have a misted, oily look* as he sits before his whiskey bottles (125). When Tyrone comes back inside after hiding from Jamie on the porch, his dressing gown is wet with fog, his collar turned up around his throat. Like Mary, the men in the Tyrone family are on intimate terms with the fog. They, too, crave its promised relief as they drift toward the shroud of forgetfulness.

To Edmund, the fog suggests the ultimate void, but even more painfully, it describes for him the death-in-life of his mother's condition: "You die—that is, inside you—and have to go on living as a ghost" (131). Edmund's own recently diagnosed illness adds to his despair. At moments he leans toward death, and that is precisely why he loves the fog: "The fog was where I wanted to be. . . . It felt damned peaceful to be nothing more than a ghost within a ghost" (131). He is comforted by the morbid thought that the fog has the capability of wiping from view the cottage and its inhabitants. In this sense, the fog, which is the most evocative element of O'Neill's set, threatens to dissolve it. Like sleep, the fog surrounds the house in darkness and invites the characters inside to dream as they journey toward night.

DRAMATIC STRUCTURE

They are not long, the days of wine and roses:
Out of a misty dream
Our path emerges for a while, then closes
Within a dream.[33]

The lines are those of the nineteenth-century British poet Ernest Dowson as quoted by Edmund in act 4 (130), and they suggest the source of O'Neill's haunting title for the play: "Long Day's Journey into Night." The Tyrones' day is a long one and contains no roses, but appropriately it is mist-enshrouded, moving out of the dim obscurity of one night and proceeding in measured pace toward the foggy gloom of another. Dowson's poem declares that our lives seem but a day surrounded on both ends by darkness and uncertainty. Tyrone prefers Shakespeare's phrasing, but the sentiment expressed is similar—life is but a dream. The thought is ancient. Extending the metaphor in time and space, O'Neill's journey into night suggests a vision of human experience as transitory. However, the play's poetic blend of haziness and retrograde motion, as its present continually dissolves into its past, presents a difficult challenge for the stage. The deliberate pace of the play (reflected in its pervasive imagery of fog and dreams) creates a languid atmosphere that would seem to be at odds with the normal requirements of drama. Dire threats, multiple incidents, rapid changes, a variety of colorful sets, last-minute revelations, and clever unravelings—*Long Day's Journey into Night* offers none of these. The play spurns the traditional manipulative devices of the stage.

There is barely a plot to speak of, if by plot we mean the arrangement of incidents in a sequence designed to keep an audience in suspense. Rather, incidents in the play are arranged in relation to criteria of internal coherence. As we grow absorbed in the lives of the four characters, we come to know as much about them as they do themselves. We discover that for the Tyrones, very little that occurs on this day is really new. Edmund is diagnosed as having tuberculosis, and Mary succumbs to her addiction: these are the crucial plot developments, and they are intertwined. Tyrone is condemned for hiring the cheap quack who administered too much morphine to Mary after Edmund's birth. If Edmund's birth started Mary on drugs, the possibility of his death now causes her relapse. We learn that her conscience also is troubled by her sense of having failed her second child, Eugene, who died in infancy when he contracted measles from Jamie. Before the play is half over, these crucial plot developments are disclosed. By the end of the second act, the audience knows most of the salient facts about the family's history, including the circumstances surrounding Eugene's death, the clues to Jamie's destructiveness, the connection between Edmund's birth and Mary's condition, and the cost of Tyrone's miserliness. The rest of the play delves more deeply into the past. Some plays aim for the shock of recognition; *Long Day's Journey into Night* gradually suffuses recognition throughout the action. It is a triumph of O'Neill's technique that audiences can be held by up to four hours of dramatic dialogue with so little promise of surprise.

If the plot moves toward the past, how does O'Neill organize his dramatic material in the present? In his *Work Diary* O'Neill toys with the possibility of employing an "orchestral technique" for *Long Day's Journey into Night,* and it appears that in composing the work he carried out this plan.[34] Some years earlier, the playwright had expressed interest in experimenting with a symphonic dramatic structure "to do what music does (to express an essentially poetic viewpoint of life) using rhythm of recurrent themes."[35] Like a symphony, the dramatic structure of *Long Day's Journey into Night* is dependent on recurring motifs. The most obvious patterns are those associated with Mary, such as her love of the fog or her fussing with her hands and hair. Other motifs for each character include reiterated topics of argument, physical gestures, speech habits, and highly slanted versions of the past.[36] By the third act the audience is familiar enough with each character's idiosyncracies to anticipate that character's responses. With each repetition of a pattern, the play advances incrementally, and the audience gains a deeper insight into the family dynamic. The monologues of the fourth and final act build upon the earlier refrains just as a well-constructed symphony might resolve its motifs in a swelling last movement during which the composer braids several melodic lines to arrive at a crescendo.

O'Neill's orchestral technique explains in part the play's substantial length. (The average playing time of the uncut version runs from three-and-a-half to four hours.) Considerable time is required to establish the play's motifs and to involve the audience intimately with the family. Indeed, on occasion O'Neill deliberately slows the rhythm of disclosure by having the characters interrupt each other at strategic moments. If interruptions are important to the play, so are repetitions. Mary highlights their importance during an exchange with Edmund in act 3. Edmund complains about his father's continual harping on his childhood poverty: "Oh, for Pete's sake, Mama. I've heard Papa tell that machine shop story ten thousand times." "Yes, dear," she replies, "You've had to listen, but I don't think you've ever tried to understand" (117). When Edmund does hear that story again in act 4, his attitude changes. For the first time he begins to understand the forces that have shaped his father's character: "I'm glad you've told me this, Papa. I know you a lot better now" (151). Edmund's reaction to his father mirrors the position of the audience listening in the theater. O'Neill insists on repetition because he wants the audience to do more than merely listen to his characters' justifications. He hopes that we, too, after several exposures, will try to understand.

THE FAMILY DYNAMIC

Shifting alliances constantly undermine any prospect for family unity. When two family members are alone, they tend to quarrel. A third person usually intervenes to restore order—but then is as likely as the original participants to renew the argument. Often Mary is the peace-maker. She intervenes on Jamie's behalf with Tyrone and on Tyrone's behalf with Jamie, but neither gesture prevents her from attacking both men later on. Similarly, Edmund defends his mother against Jamie in act 1 but later throws Jamie's charges in her face. A strategy employed by each family member is to attack another's point of greatest vulnerability. When Mary accuses Tyrone of stinginess, he counters with the charge that she is behaving like Jamie by attributing the lowest of motives to others (85). That in turn reminds Mary of Jamie's suspicions of her own behavior, and she backs off.

The Tyrones exhibit patterns typical of families in which chemical dependency is a serious problem. Their interactions are characterized by denial, suspicion, insecurity, guilt, isolation, and resentment. Members of such families often blame themselves for the behavior of the addict or alcoholic, or they become codependents in denial and risk addiction themselves. Frequent disappointment leads to mistrust and suspicion, and eventually such families become isolated from social contact in the community. The children in particular seethe with anger. They strive to make peace with themselves, their siblings and parents, but their resentment constantly boils to the surface and finds expression in a generally bitter attitude toward life.

The distinctive pattern in the Tyrone family is to attack and then withdraw. In act 1, for example, Jamie sneers with jealousy at his father's pride in Edmund's exploits: "And what did his going away get him? Look at him now!" (35). Immediately, he regrets this remark. Shamefaced, he apologizes: "Christ! That's a lousy thing to say" (35). A moment later, he is on the attack again, with another snide remark about Edmund's journalism. Then, ashamed once more, he takes back his words a second time. Next he tries to praise Edmund but undercuts himself yet again, and finally he drops the subject altogether. Deflecting his hostility, he loses his temper, apologizes for this new outburst, and then moves to explore with Tyrone whatever common ground they are willing to share on the subject of Mary.

As a family the Tyrones are driven by strongly opposing impulses. They hunger for intimacy and yet dread it. Consider the following sequence, which occurs at the beginning of act 4, just as Edmund arrives home. First, Tyrone frowns and calls in a quarrelsome tone: "Turn out that light before you come in." Then, relieved that he has company, he softens: "I'm glad you've come, lad. I've been damned lonely." Then, "*resentfully*," he berates Edmund for leaving him alone (126)—all in the space of a few seconds. To mask their emotions, each member of the family adopts a disingenuous pose. Tyrone typically projects false heartiness, Jamie shrugs to disguise his pain, Edmund chuckles derisively, and Mary tries to tease. Over the course of the play, these masks dissolve. On at least two occasions, Mary breaks into tears, and so do Tyrone and Jamie. Edmund blinks back tears in act 4.

When the Tyrones do allow their emotions to surface, they can be demonstrative. Jamie habitually takes Edmund by the arm to draw him closer, and in act 4, Edmund pats Jamie on the arm to comfort him—a noteworthy gesture since no one else in the family ever touches Jamie. In act 1, Edmund takes Mary's hand, and in act 2 he impulsively gives his father an affectionate hug, which Tyrone returns (91). At one point Tyrone suddenly hugs Mary. She kisses her husband "*gratefully*" in act 1 (41), and throws her arms around him, sobbing, in act 3 (122). In act 1 she also kisses Edmund tenderly (43). Later, though, Edmund remains sullenly unyielding in her presence, once taking her hand and then dropping it, "*overcome by bitterness*" (119). Both her son and her husband turn from Mary as the signs of her addiction reappear, and when she greets them at the door in the middle of the third act, they "*submit shrinkingly*" (108). These physical gestures serve to underscore both the closeness of the Tyrone family and their mutual fears of contact.

For the Tyrones, the most significant question during the day is whether to forgive or to forget. To deny the past would be to deny their common history, which is why Edmund wages a campaign to keep the past alive. Unless they remember the past, he argues, there can be no hope for the future. But Tyrone continually urges the family to forget. For Mary, it would be soothing to forget, because remembering humiliates her. At a crucial point during their argument in act 3, Tyrone cries pleadingly: "Mary! Can't you forget—?" "No, dear," she replies. "But I forgive" (114). It is her finest moment. If Mary remembers and forgives, no matter how deep the grievance, then the family unit can remain strong. But as night approaches, Mary annihilates the present by retreating hopelessly into the past—she over-remembers, as it were—and then the family seems lost. In a letter to a friend, O'Neill interpreted the ending of the play: "At the final curtain, there they still are, trapped within each other by the past, each guilty and at the same time innocent, scorning, loving, pitying each other, understanding, and yet not understanding at all, forgiving but still doomed never to be able to forget."[37]

That the word "forget" appears twice as many times in the play as the word "forgive" graphically describes the family dynamic. A similar word count discloses that "love" is mentioned on more than sixty occasions and "hate" on fewer than thirty (a parallel ratio of two to one). These numbers only confirm what any responsive audience intuitively knows about the Tyrones. As Jamie tells Edmund in act 4, "I love you more than I hate you" (166). That same love/hate ratio extends throughout the family and is replicated in every pairing. The dynamic tension between love and hate is the binding force that keeps the Tyrone family together.

WHOSE PLAY IS IT?
THE PARENTS

===== 5 =====

EDMUND: Whose play is it?

TYRONE: I don't know. Mine, I guess. No, it's yours.
               —*Long Day's Journey into Night,* act 4

During their card game in act 4, Edmund and his father exchange a casual pleasantry that raises an interesting critical issue in *Long Day's Journey into Night.* Whose play is it? Which of the four major characters is the central figure in the drama? For most plays this question never needs to be asked: the protagonist is obvious. He or she is the dominant personality and is usually responsible for the play's major problem. The protagonist suffers the consequences, occupies center stage, and in the process gains most of our attention and sympathy. According to these principles, *Death of a Salesman* is Willy Loman's play. *Hamlet* is Hamlet's. *A Streetcar Named Desire* belongs to Blanche Dubois. But whose play is *Long Day's Journey into Night?* A case might be made for each of the four Tyrones. One reason that the play is so engrossing is that each family member can be seen as the central axis around which the drama turns.

For instance, Mary dominates the stage by claiming the largest

The playwright's mother, Mary Ellen ("Ella") Quinlan O'Neill, as a young woman. Photograph courtesy of the Collection of American Literature, Beinecke Rare Book and Manuscript Library, Yale University.

share of our attention, with a scene to herself and a significant speech ending each of the four acts. Yet the family bitterly argues that James bears the main burden of responsibility for their unhappiness. His fourth-act monologue, which is meant to redeem him, is the dramatic climax of the play. Is Tyrone, then, cut more closely to the pattern of the typical tragic hero, a flawed figure whose actions unintentionally cause the suffering of others? Then again, no character suffers more desperately than Jamie, or is quite as reliable at uncovering the truth. From that perspective, a case might be made for Jamie as protagonist. Finally, Edmund is the character who most readily gains our sympathy, and it is through his eyes that we tend to judge the other members of the family. Is Edmund therefore the main focus of interest in the play? This deceptively simple question—Whose play is it?—cannot be answered easily.

MARY TYRONE

Mary's collapse poses the greatest threat to the Tyrone family, and in this regard she acts as the pivot of the play. The most salient feature of Mary's behavior is her slide into drug addiction. However, morphine is not her only problem. Mary Tyrone has suffered a number of losses in her life, and she has not coped well with any of them. She has lost her parents (her father at an early age) and her baby, Eugene—the most severe blow of all. Now her elder son is lost to alcohol and her younger is threatened by tuberculosis, the same disease that carried off her father. According to her own testimony, Mary has lost her youth, her dreams, her faith, and her "true self." "At last everything comes between you and what you'd like to be, and you've lost your true self forever" (61). Although Mary's plaintive cry is prompted by her addiction, it also seems to embrace a wider frame of reference. At no point in her life has Mary Cavan Tyrone ever been firmly in control.

When Mary staggers into the living room at the end of the fourth act, she is a woman in search of her past. But her losses have been so various that she cannot focus clearly on any of them. What is it that she is looking for? Her long soliloquy is framed around a hazy search for that one particular possession whose loss would be more insupportable than any other. Her final line brings its discovery: "Yes, I remember. I fell in love with James Tyrone" (176). In other words, Mary's "true self" is bound as intimately to her memory of early happiness with James as it is to her religious longing or to the recovery of her willpower. If sometimes she thinks that meeting Tyrone was the beginning of her troubles, Mary also realizes that nothing in her life has been more important to her than his support. "I know you still love me, James, in spite of everything," she tells him in act 3 (112). Tyrone's love is one of the few important things in life that Mary has retained.

True, Mary accuses him of not understanding her, of drinking too much, of depriving her of friends and a decent home, and of making Jamie into a "boozer." Yet in spite of everything, she resolutely defends him against criticism from his sons. She implores Edmund "to understand and forgive him, too, and not feel contempt because he's close-fisted" (117). For thirty-six years she has loved Tyrone "under the circumstances" (114), for she believes that like everyone else, he "can't help being what he is" (101). Although sometimes Mary regards her husband as an antagonist, she also sees in him a mirror image of her flawed self: a romantic figure, lovable but weak, a helpless victim of life.

Upon her entrance O'Neill describes Mary as a middle-aged woman with distinctively Irish features, a full, youthful figure, large, beautiful eyes, and thick, pure white hair. "*Her most appealing quality is the simple, unaffected charm of the shy convent-girl youthfulness she has never lost—an innate worldly innocence*" (13). Yet at the same time, we are struck by her extreme nervousness. Throughout the play Mary fidgets self-consciously with her hair. Her once beautiful hands, now knotted by rheumatism, flutter upwards, as constant reminders of her waning charm. Glimmers of the convent girl return when Mary is under the influence of morphine. There is an "*uncanny gay, free youthfulness in her manner*" in act 3 (97), and by act 4, she has sunk deep into her schoolgirlish pose, her white hair braided in pigtails as she relives her conversation with Mother Elizabeth.

Mary's pose of innocence is a mask that protects her from the despair that has consumed her adulthood. There is never any doubt as to the origin of Mary's addiction. "If you'd spent money for a decent doctor when she was so sick after I was born," Edmund screams at his father, "she'd never have known morphine existed!" (140). However, the fault is not all Tyrone's. Mary's successive relapses after a number of supposed "cures" suggest an ongoing drive for escape that impels her toward self-destruction. Even before her first knowledge of morphine, Mary's attitude toward Edmund's birth was clouded by refusal: "I was afraid all the time I carried Edmund. I knew something terrible would happen" (88). In her guilt over Eugene's accidental death, Mary anticipated some fateful consequence if she were to conceive another child. As a result, she believes, Edmund was born nervous and too sensitive, and his present illness seems to her a working out of some terrible curse for which she feels responsible. Her father's death, Eugene's death, Edmund's birth, her own addiction, Edmund's illness— all these dire fears and memories come crowding in on Mary during the day, driving her to the spare room and her cache of drugs.

When in the play does Mary actually lose control? Jamie suspects that his mother started her injections the previous night, when he heard her moving about in the spare room. However, several critics have suggested that Mary's fall occurs around lunchtime or during the interlude between acts 1 and 2. Törnqvist makes a strong case for the latter possibility, reasoning that Mary is motivated by the unjustified suspicions of the men during the first act.[38] But O'Neill leaves the question unresolved. In his notes for the play he indicates that Mary has not yet taken her first shot before the curtain rises, but in the scenario it seems that she has. In the final text, it is early in act 2 that *"Jamie knows after one probing look at her that his suspicions are justified"* (58), but even before that, during the late morning in act 1, the men stare at Mary with a growing dread. It is not entirely clear whether Mary begins her injections during the night, in the morning, or shortly before or after lunch. However, there is no doubt that by the second act the effects of her clandestine treatment have become noticeable. The stage directions used most frequently to describe her

reactions are "*detached*," "*strangely*," "*defensively*," and "*dreamily*."
On fifteen different occasions Mary tries to force a smile or a laugh,
but no one is fooled. By early afternoon her battle is lost.

Act 3 concentrates almost exclusively on Mary. As the curtain
goes up, a moan of the foghorn is heard, and Mary is discovered in a
disheveled state, her eyes shining with unnatural brilliance. The effects
of morphine on her behavior have become pronounced. The men are
away in town, so Mary is able to share an intimate moment with
Cathleen, the only member of the household who is not also part of
the family. Mary has no woman friend in whom to confide, so she is
reduced to sharing her most intimate memories with a blank-looking
servant who understands very little and who responds with trivialities.
Yet Cathleen is more than a sounding board; she is a buffer between
Mary and the outside world. It is Cathleen who carries Mary's prescriptions into the drugstore and who suffers the scowling disapproval
of the town's pharmacist (103). Through Cathleen we glimpse Mary
much as the town sees her. Cathleen's position in the household also
parallels Mary's in that they both are subject to the demands of others.
(In Cathleen's case, Bridget the cook orders her about, and Smythe the
chauffeur is too free with his hands.) Mary feels compatible with
Cathleen, drawn to her, perhaps, because of their mutual powerless-
ness. But even though Mary shares her happiest memories with Cathleen, she waits until she is alone again to voice her deepest thoughts
(107). When the men unburden themselves in act 4, each has a listening companion to lend a sympathetic ear. In contrast, Mary confesses
alone, her isolation complete.

In light of her situation, Mary's professed code of blamelessness is
largely a cover for her sense of shame. "It's wrong to blame your
brother," she tells Edmund. "He can't help being what the past has
made him. Any more than your father can. Or you. Or I" (64). Her
tolerance is self-serving: as one who believes she has lost her soul
through drugs, she herself most needs forgiveness. Moreover, Mary's
attacks on the family seem to be spurred by her own defensiveness.
Even in the midst of self-accusation, she cannot help deflecting guilt
upon others. The most glaring example of this maneuver occurs in the

second act when Mary recalls the circumstances surrounding the death of Eugene.

> I blame myself only. I swore after Eugene died I would never have another baby. I was to blame for his death. If I hadn't left him with my mother to join you on the road, because you wrote telling me you missed me and were so lonely, Jamie would never have been allowed, when he still had measles, to go into the baby's room. *Her face hardening.* I've always believed Jamie did it on purpose. (87)

Mary begins her confession by assuming the blame herself, but then almost immediately slides it toward her mother and then Tyrone. Finally she lodges it squarely on Jamie's shoulders, in effect recanting her first statement. Mary repeats the pattern as she continues: "It was my fault. I should have insisted on staying with Eugene and not have let you persuade me to join you, just because I loved you" (88). It was my fault because I loved you—in other words, it was *your* fault. At such moments Mary is a dangerous, destructive presence in the family. We can imagine her telling Jamie over the years that he is not accountable for his brother's death, while on each occasion riddling him with guilt.[39]

As the day progresses, Mary's hostility toward her accusers becomes more overt. Toward Jamie she feels especially spiteful. In violation of her own code of forgiveness, she continues to blame him for Eugene's death. She also fears him because he is always the first to guess her condition when she resorts to drugs: "He's always sneering . . . looking for the worst weakness in everyone" (61). Mary, scornful of Jamie's drinking, claims that he has disgraced the family and will drag Edmund down with him until Edmund is "as hopeless a failure as he is" (109). Although she does not desire this result, her rejection of Jamie effectively has destroyed him. Throughout the play he feels rebuffed by her and hurt.

Mary's feelings toward Edmund are more complicated. She dotes on him, but at the same time she feels that it was his birth that led to her addiction. At times she wishes that he never had been born: "It would have been better for his sake" (122). As usual, Mary mixes her solicitude for Edmund with her own feelings of inadequacy. Twice during the play she insists that she is not using Edmund to excuse her reliance on drugs, but she fails to be convincing. On several occasions Mary belittles Edmund in her anxiety over his health, denying that he is really sick at all. In so doing, she refuses Edmund's genuine need for her sympathy, much as she tried to deny him as a child. "It's as if, in spite of loving us, she hated us!" Edmund blurts out at last (139), and there is truth in his remark. In a sense Mary regards her family as she does her crippled hands. They are blighted appendages that provoke the need for painkiller: "They're far away. I see them, but the pain is gone" (104).

For Mary, "The past is the present, isn't it? It's the future, too" (87). So that we may understand her background, O'Neill subtly provides enough information to permit us to reconstruct Mary's past in some detail. From scattered references, the following portrait emerges of her youth. As a young girl, Mary Cavan was spoiled by her father, who would do anything she asked. He pampered her, paid for special music lessons, and would have sent her to Europe to study the piano had she not fallen in love with Tyrone. He was the one who introduced her to Tyrone and who provided a lavish wedding. That Mary passed directly from her father's hands into those of his friend suggests that she never had time to develop strong interests of her own or to explore the independence that comes with autonomous living. This fact from Mary's past helps explain her attitude toward her husband. Mary idealizes her father and at first probably associated Tyrone with his exaggerated virtues, in particular, his generosity. Then as time wore on, she could not help but to compare Tyrone unfavorably with her father, who died young, leaving all her illusions about him intact. Tyrone suggests as much: "Her father wasn't the great, generous, noble Irish gentleman that she makes out" (137). He was "a nice enough man" but no hero, and like his daughter and her future husband, he too had a weakness. He drank himself to death on champagne, aggravated by consumption. Mary condemns Tyrone's drinking but represses the memory of her father's alcoholism. Instead, her memory of her father is frozen in a child's image of parental doting. Even now she cannot see him as he was, nor note the unpalatable family resemblance between the Cavans and the Tyrones.

In contrast to the father who adored her, Mary remembers her mother as cold and withdrawn. Perhaps, she thinks, her mother was even a little jealous of her (114). Although Mary's father encouraged her marriage, her mother opposed it, predicting that her daughter was too spoiled to ever make a good wife.[40] Instead, she hoped that Mary would become a nun. Mary's impulse more than likely was to rebel against her mother's opinion of her inadequacy as a woman—and what better way to defy her than to prove that she could attract a man who resembled her own father in outward ways? Given these circumstances, it is likely that Mary Cavan approached her marriage to Tyrone with unrealistic expectations. At the beginning, their union fulfilled Mary's naive and exaggerated hopes, but after the deaths of her father and Eugene, and in the aftermath of Edmund's birth, Mary's view of the marriage soured. Now, in middle age, she has turned her back on the role of wife and mother. In *Long Day's Journey into Night* Mary retreats through morphine to a state of preadulthood, adopting the guise of the virginal convent girl that her rejecting mother had urged upon her when she was an adolescent.

Mary remembers her convent days with genuine fondness. There the nuns continued to spoil her, flattering her and making her their pet. In Mother Elizabeth she found a replacement for her biological mother who was cold and distant. And in Sister Martha, who ran the infirmary, she found a source of relief for pains and cares: Sister Martha always had "things in her medicine chest" that would cure any hurt (171). During this period in her life Mary formed her two most important dreams: "To be a nun, that was the more beautiful one. To become a concert pianist, that was the other" (104). Neither of these dreams, it appears, was realistic. According to Tyrone, Mary played the piano well enough for a schoolgirl, but her potential to become a professional pianist was limited. As for her second, more beautiful dream, Cathleen bluntly observes: "I can't imagine you a holy nun, Ma'am" (102). Tyrone agrees that Mary was never meant to renounce the world, and apparently Mother Elizabeth thought so too, sending Mary home to reconsider, to "prove it wasn't simply my imagination" (175). Tyrone remembers Mary at that age as "a bit of a rogue and a coquette" (138), and Mary herself recalls with pleasure her physical attractiveness.

Indeed, Mary Cavan, according to her own account, was always "dreaming and forgetting" (171). Soon she had a third dream that swept aside the other two. It was to marry James Tyrone, the famous matinee idol who reminded her of her father. Mary's description of her first meeting with Tyrone is cloaked in the mist of schoolgirl romanticism. She first saw the actor backstage after his performance in a play about the French Revolution, surrounded by all the trappings of make-believe: "And he was handsomer than my wildest dream, in his make-up and his nobleman's costume. . .like someone from another world. . .All I wanted was to be his wife" (105). Like a wish in a fairy tale, Mary's third dream came true—and then life exacted its payment. Captured by the magic of Tyrone's performance, Mary could not accept the backstage grime of theatrical living, which she grew to detest. The pattern of her attraction to dreaming repeats itself in the present through Mary's attempts to ward off reality. Now only morphine and the fog can offer the solace that she seeks.[41]

For Mary the theater itself has become a symbol of life's disappointment. Never has she felt at home in the theater or with the people in James's company. She believes the theater keeps her from having a respectable home. She regards the cottage as a shabby summer place where she is embarrassed to receive guests. Since her marriage, Mary has lived in trains, a broken-down cabin, theaters, and second-rate hotels. Sometimes she thinks that her mistake in life was to marry an actor and to be drawn behind the scenes. "Women used to wait at the stage door just to see him come out," she recalls (105). But Mary entered the stage door, and once she crossed that threshold of illusion, she found that the magic of the theater was destroyed.

Now, at fifty-four, she feels old and desperate. Romance is gone, and little in life awaits her. Once already Mary has tried to commit suicide: she screamed for morphine and ran out of the house in her nightdress to throw herself off the dock (86). She thinks of suicide again during this gloomy afternoon: "I hope, sometime, without meaning it, I will take an overdose. I never could do it deliberately. The Blessed Virgin would never forgive me, then" (121). If only she could regain her faith, she thinks, then she could pray again; and then she might discover the strength to break the soul-stealing habit that has turned her life of schoolgirl dreaming into a nightmare.

JAMES TYRONE

If the theater to Mary means the opposite of a home, to James it has meant the alternative to the poorhouse. Twice his fatherless family was evicted from their hovel, and the misery he suffered as a child has shaped his personality to a profound degree. There was no romance in his poverty, he tells Edmund, but both romance and money beckoned in the theater. Trading on his good looks, the young man seized his opportunity, beginning as an extra and rising to stardom. Mary complains that their cottage is no better than a poorhouse, everything about it being so cheaply done, but Tyrone cannot help cutting corners. He knows the difference between economy and destitution, which remains his abject fear: he worries that his "final curtain will be in the poorhouse just the same, and that's not comedy!" (128).

Tyrone is a man of startling contradictions. He has spent a lifetime on stage clothed in resplendent costumes, while at home he dresses shabbily in a threadbare suit. He squanders thousands on worthless property and stints on furnishings for the house. To his family he is no longer a swashbuckling hero but an embarrassment. His once mellifluous stage voice now is reduced to snarls and grumbles: what we first learn about the former matinee idol is that he snores. Still, "*the stamp of his profession is unmistakably on him*" (13). Tyrone's gestures, habits of speech, movement, and his upright bearing, which makes him appear taller than he is, all "*have the quality of belonging to a studied technique*" (13). Even at home the actor prides himself on his entrances and exits: Tyrone always keeps the family waiting at mealtimes. While trimming the hedge, he bows to the Chatfields, who pass by, as if he were taking a curtain call. Mary can tell when he is acting, and so can his sons. Edmund refers to his father's histrionic pose at the chandelier as "a grand curtain," and the stage directions confirm that Tyrone turns on the three bulbs with "*dramatic self-pity*" (128). But Tyrone is not always "on." At the beginning of the last act, we discover him wearing his pince-nez, dressed in an old robe, playing solitaire, "*a sad, defeated old man, possessed by hopeless resignation*" (125).

Despite past successes, Tyrone is driven by insecurity. The first indication that his thrift is compulsive occurs in the opening moments of the play when he reaches for a cheap cigar and brags about his bargain. His casual remark sparks the first argument of the day, as Mary acidly shifts the subject to his so-called "bargains" in real estate. Tyrone's behavior with money is paradoxical. In the barroom he is profligate, standing rounds for strangers, whereas at home he keeps his whiskey padlocked in the cellar. He has loaned money to deadbeats who would never pay it back, but he is also more generous with his sons than either will admit. After all, he supports them both and has been influential in getting them the few irregular jobs that they have held. He pays for a cook, a maid, and a chauffeur to ease Mary's days and to distract her. It may be the case that he pays cheap wages and scouts out secondhand bargains, but in peculiar ways Tyrone belies his reputation as the complete skinflint.

What damns him is that he is tightfisted about essentials, especially medical care. On this point Jamie blames his father's fatalism: "What I'm afraid of is, with your Irish bogtrotter idea that consumption is fatal, you'll figure it would be a waste of money to spend any more [on Edmund] than you can help" (80). And Tyrone does reason in this manner (33). In act 4 Edmund repeats the charge that his father is sending him to a "bargain" sanatorium because he believes that Edmund is going to die. The pattern is repeated in Tyrone's attitude toward Mary's addiction: "I've spent thousands upon thousands in cures! A waste!" (141). The hiring of a cheap hotel doctor to attend Mary during Edmund's birth is but another stitch in this design. At the root of Tyrone's compulsiveness is a superstitious double attitude.

When he expects the worst, he is a miser. When he expects the best, he is a gambler, a "sucker for every con man with a gold mine" (141).

No matter how well we understand Tyrone, it is a shock to learn that he allows McGuire to "stick" him with another piece of bad property on the very day that he wrangles with Hardy over the choice of a sanatorium for Edmund. When Edmund catches his father in a lie about this transaction, he explodes with outrage. The episode is even more damning because Jamie had predicted it in act 1. Tyrone is brought to the nadir of disgrace, yet this exposure motivates his most important speech, in which he describes to Edmund the poverty of his youth: "A stinking old miser. Well, maybe you're right. Maybe I can't help being [one]" (146).

Although he pretends to reject his wife's fatalism, Tyrone does agree with Mary that the past determines the present and the future, too. To Edmund he denies that destiny controls human actions, quoting easily from his store of Shakespeare: "The fault, dear Brutus, is not in our stars, but in ourselves that we are underlings" (152). However, Tyrone is speaking not from his heart but from a text. (The line belongs to Cassius in *Julius Caesar,* a part that Tyrone played earlier in his career.) Now he seems to be playing the role of the stern father who feels it his duty to rebuke his son's cynicism. On the occasions when Tyrone does relax into his own voice, he unconsciously echoes Mary's sentiments. For both, life is a personal antagonist who eventually gains the upper hand after bestowing deceptive gifts.

Certainly the circumstances of Tyrone's childhood were appalling: an irresponsible father who deserted the family when the boy was ten; a mother who kept the children together by scrubbing floors, whose constant worry (which she passed on to her son) was that her days would end in the poorhouse; early responsibility, with a sister and two younger brothers to feed; real, grinding hunger; inadequate clothing; and instead of school, a crushing job in a machine shop, where for twelve hours a day and fifty cents a week he labored to make files. Maybe, Tyrone explains, "life overdid the lesson for me, and made a dollar worth too much" (149). Tyrone's escape from the machine shop to the theater must have seemed to him as miraculous as the Count of

Monte Cristo's escape from Château d'If. Perhaps it never seemed entirely real. For a time, at least, the world was his. When Booth praised his talent, he looked forward to a promising artistic career, but a few years later he found the big money-maker, and then the tables turned. The road show was another one of Tyrone's disastrous "bargains": it ruined him with its promise of an easy fortune and eventually cost him his career as a Shakespearean actor. "Then," Tyrone concludes, "life had me where it wanted me," and it was too late to change (150). None of us, Mary says, can help the things life does to us. Deep down, Tyrone believes that, too.

In a sense, the lives of James and Mary have followed an identical course. Both had a favorite parent and a distant one; the parent each idolized was of the opposite sex. Perhaps their subsequent disappointment in each other as marriage partners owes something to the unrealistic expectation each had that the other could serve as a replacement for the favorite parent who died. Similarly, both have been frustrated in their dreams of careers. Mary's early enthusiasm for the piano matches Tyrone's abiding love for Shakespeare. Mary: "I used to love the piano. I worked so hard at my music in the convent—if you can call it work when you do something you love" (103). Tyrone: "I would have acted in any of his plays for nothing, for the joy of being alive in his great poetry" (150). Mary glows when recalling her music teacher's praise of her talent, just as Tyrone does in recalling Booth's praise of his. Like most women of her day, Mary finally chose to make marriage her career, and the highlight of her memories concerns her wedding gown. The "high spot" in Tyrone's career was his performance as Othello. Tyrone recalls that he had the theater manager put Booth's praise down in writing, and as night descends, he wonders what has become of his memento. Ironically, Edmund perceives the parallel between his parents when he wonders if the paper is lying along with Mary's wedding dress in an old trunk in the attic. In their soliloquies Mary and Tyrone express similar wistfulness and uncertainty. "What is it I'm looking for?" Mary wonders as she descends the stairs (172). "What the hell was it I wanted to buy?" asks Tyrone (150). Both parents punctuate their lives with question marks.

Because they have already shared so many disappointments, Tyrone is able to steel himself at the first sign of Mary's relapse. He bears toward Mary a stoical attitude compounded of pity, disapproval, and resignation. But Tyrone is no martyr and cannot help wounding Mary for the pain she causes. Even in the opening scene, his compliments about how well she looks and how glad they all are to have her home again might be unconscious barbs, reminders of Mary's previous backsliding. Tyrone is capable of angry outbursts, too: they could have had a home, he argues, had it not been for Mary's instability. At such moments, though, he usually catches himself and relents, deciding that Mary is not responsible for her addiction. As the situation deteriorates, he makes an effort to soften his tone toward Mary and urges her to forget the past. Throughout the play he comforts her physically, at the beginning placing his hand *"over one of her nervously playing ones"* (17), and at the end holding her wedding dress *"in his arms with an unconscious, clumsy protective gentleness"* (172). Ultimately Tyrone knows that he cannot protect his wife, and his helplessness hurts his pride.

Tyrone's relationship with his sons is strained. He begrudges Edmund's pampered upbringing when compared with his own and expects more gratitude than he receives. Yet in the fourth act he and Edmund discover that they share a common dream, a vision of artistic integrity. By contrast, Jamie, who never has had "a loftier dream than whores and whiskey" (129), is written off completely by his father. On this night Tyrone hopes that Jamie will miss the last trolley home and be forced to stay uptown. Perhaps the old actor's bitterness toward Jamie is intensified by seeing his own artistic failure mirrored by his namesake. In his drunkenness, Jamie bawls: "Look in my face. My name is Might-Have-Been" (168). Tyrone describes his own career in nearly identical terms, confiding to Edmund that he would be willing to enter the poorhouse in his old age if only he could look back "on having been the fine artist I might have been" (151).

Tyrone is described most often in the stage directions as angry, scowling, resentful, bitter, guilty, helpless, and contemptuous. O'Neill flavors his personality by a range of colorful traits that bring him vividly to life. His robust health, for example, is commented upon on several occasions. Tyrone looks ten years younger than his actual age of sixty-five; he claims to have the lungs of an ox and the digestion of a man of twenty. "*There is a lot of stolid, earthy peasant in him,*" we are told (13). He has an enormous appetite, sleeps well, snores heavily, and enjoys cigars and whiskey with few apparent ill effects. He consumes a great deal of alcohol during the day, but in contrast to Jamie, he never loses command of himself. He insists that he has never missed a performance in his life. Tyrone's iron constitution is actually a cause of friction in the household because it makes him less tolerant of weakness and ill health in others. He cannot identify with Edmund's condition or Mary's lack of control when she is under the influence of morphine.

Tyrone also is fiercely proud of his Irish heritage and religion. Shakespeare and the Duke of Wellington, he asserts (without evidence) were Irish Catholics; Edmund ribs him mercilessly on this score. He may not be a regular churchgoer, but James takes his faith seriously, in contrast to his sons, who are apostates. "When you deny God," he is fond of saying, "you deny hope" (134). The idea of suicide violates his faith and appalls him; it is difficult for him to acknowledge that both his wife and his son have recently attempted to end their lives. When Edmund recalls his suicide attempt, Tyrone protests that no son of his "would ever—"; then he breaks off, swallowing the recollection that his own father may have taken rat poison after he returned to Ireland (147). Tyrone is more sensitive to criticism than the others and is frequently "*overwhelmed by shame which he tries to hide*" (113). Here, too, his religion plays a role, shaping his sense of moral duty and responsibility.

Cathleen observes of Tyrone: "Well, he's a fine, handsome, kind gentleman, just the same, Ma'am. Never mind his weakness" (101). Edmund agrees: "I'm like Mama. I can't help liking you, in spite of everything" (142). Only Jamie hangs back: "What a bastard to have for a father! Christ, if you put him in a book, no one would believe it!" (157). In Jamie's remark, O'Neill seems to be posing a private challenge to himself as a writer. O'Neill did put his father in a book—and treated him with charity. Of the many characters he created during a long and productive career as a playwright, James Tyrone is one of the most credible and engaging.

WHOSE PLAY IS IT?
THE SONS

$$==== 6 ====$$

"Greater love hath no man than this, that he saveth his brother from himself."

—Jamie, *Long Day's Journey into Night*, act 4

JAMES TYRONE, JR.

James and Mary transmit the family legacy; Edmund and Jamie inherit it. Edmund looks to the future, but Jamie is anchored to the past. He is the blighted Tyrone. Two themes darkly stain his life: his intense rivalry with each male in the family and his fatal dependency on his mother. In a typical judgment of his son, Tyrone snaps at him about hedge cutting: "You'd get it crooked, as you get everything else" (81).

Throughout the play Jamie is compared unfavorably with his father. Tyrone looks younger than his sixty-five years; Jamie looks much older than his thirty-three. Signs of premature disintegration mar his countenance. His hair is thinning, and although he has his father's broad-shouldered build, he appears shorter and stouter. Like his father he snores, but drink and dissipation have sapped his vitality, and unlike Tyrone he appears in dubious health. When he smiles, Jamie shows traces of the irresponsible charm that makes him still attractive to women, but more often an expression of habitual cynicism *"gives his countenance a Mephistophelian cast"* (19). O'Neill's allusion suggests that Jamie inhabits a personal hell. His life has been marked by repeated failures. He has betrayed the brilliant promise of his early years and disgraced the family by his expulsions from boarding school and college. Even now he has no steady employment, depending on his father for pocket money. His temporary acting jobs are favors from his father, and thus Jamie views the theater with contempt. Every summer he slinks back to the cottage because he has no home or profession of his own, and there he endures the indignity of his parents' scorn.

What are the causes of Jamie's failure? Mary blames Tyrone for Jamie's alcoholism, citing his practice of giving the boy a teaspoonful of whiskey to quiet him whenever he had nightmares. Jamie himself traces his collapse to his discovery as a teenager that his mother was an addict: "Never forget the first time I got wise. Caught her in the act with a hypo" (163). Jamie's alcoholism is tied directly to Mary's morphine addiction: over the years his drinking has risen and fallen in relation to Mary's cures. This last time, he says, he really "believed the best." To Edmund he confesses, "I'd begun to hope, if she'd beaten the game, I could, too" (162). His claim is borne out by a stage direction early in the first act. When Tyrone kisses Mary and her face lights up with girlish charm, Jamie's face clears too, *"and there is an old boyish charm in his loving smile at his mother"* (28). But with Mary's relapse, Jamie returns to the bottle. He is like a driver in the fog blindly following the car ahead of him into disaster.

In addition to drink, Jamie's defenses against the world include mockery and sardonic humor. Fourteen times during the play he shrugs his shoulders cynically, and most of his lines are delivered in a jeering tone. Edmund remonstrates: "You're the limit! At the Last Judgment, you'll be around telling everyone it's in the bag" (165). In fact, Jamie despises himself. Although he never mentions it, the death of Eugene weighs heavily on his conscience. Mary contends that Tyrone insisted she have another baby to take Eugene's place, although she was against the idea (88). Jamie reasons that had Eugene lived, Edmund might not have been conceived, and then Mary never would have known morphine. He has shouldered this guilt since he was a little boy. Whenever the present grows intolerable, the other members of the family can look back on a happier past, but not Jamie. Mary has her convent days, Tyrone his triumph in *Othello,* Edmund his romantic adventures at sea. Each has glimpsed a moment of fulfillment and can share that vision with the family. Jamie, on the other hand, has only snatches of secondhand poetry to draw upon to validate his feelings.[42] Unlike the others, he cannot afford to dream about the past because the memory that brands his childhood is the mark of Cain.

Because he has neither past nor future to contemplate, Jamie lives exclusively in the present. He is the first to guess that Edmund has consumption, and he attempts to convince his father of that unpleasant fact early in the play. He assesses the consequences of allowing Mary to delude herself about Edmund's health and tries to prepare Edmund for the bad news that he knows is on the way from Dr. Hardy. Similarly, Jamie is the first to guess what is happening to Mary. While Edmund and Tyrone continue to deny the truth, Jamie bluntly forces them to interpret her behavior without illusion: "Another shot in the arm! . . . The truth is there is no cure and we've been saps to hope" (75–76). Since the Tyrones do not always place the highest premium on truth-telling, Jamie remains a prophet without honor in the family.

Tyrone's antagonism toward his eldest son is relentless. Jamie in return derides his father at every opportunity. To him, Tyrone is "the Old Man," "Gaspard the Miser," "a bastard," or a ham actor with no more professional dignity than a performing seal. As far as Jamie is concerned, Tyrone is to blame for everything—for his mother's addiction, for his own failed career, and even for Edmund's precarious future. "Although, in a way," he adds, in the play's most mysterious line, "I do feel sorry for him about one thing" (157). What precisely does Jamie mean by this? He never continues the thought—"But to hell with that" (157)—yet the context suggests that this allusion must have something to do with his father's relationship to his mother. The comment is a puzzlement that bears teasing out.

If Jamie means only to express sympathy with his father for having to endure Mary's condition, why should he bury the thought? Elsewhere he refers openly to their common sorrow. Perhaps Jamie is thinking of his father not merely as head of the family but as Mary's spouse who, as a result of her withdrawal, often has been deprived of the sexual connection that husbands and wives may know but which sons and mothers may not. That subject appears to be much on Jamie's mind, though he dares not speak of it directly. Indeed, there are many signs that he is bitterly jealous of his father. For example, when Jamie rouses himself from his drunken stupor in act 4, he greets Tyrone with lines from *Richard III* that suggest he secretly thinks of his father as a hated rival: "Clarence is come, false, fleeting, perjured Clarence, / That stabbed me in a field by Tewksbury" (168).[43] Jamie repeats this stabbing image in his warning to Edmund to steer clear in the future: "And when you come back, look out for me. I'll be waiting to welcome you with that 'my old pal' stuff, and give you the glad hand, and at the first good chance I get stab you in the back" (166). All his life Jamie has been competing unsuccessfully with his father for his mother's love and has transferred his feelings of rivalry to his brothers. Already he has destroyed one brother, Eugene. Now he is trying to protect his remaining brother from a similar fate at his hands.

To what extent was Jamie, at the age of seven, aware of the possible consequences of entering his baby brother's room? Mary accuses him of acting on purpose, even though he had been warned that his contagion might be fatal to Eugene. "He was jealous of the baby," Mary charges. "He hated him" (87). She also believes that Jamie bears the same attitude toward Edmund: "He's jealous because Edmund has always been the baby—just as he used to be of Eugene" (109). Whatever the truth may be about the past, Jamie's present behavior is consistent with Mary's view. In act 1 he tries to subvert his father's good opinion of his brother, and in act 4, after liquor has loosened his tongue, he confesses to Edmund that he has tried to undermine Edmund's future by introducing him to a life of whores and whiskey: "Never wanted you [to] succeed and make me look even worse by comparison. Wanted you to fail. Always jealous of you. Mama's baby, Papa's pet!" (165). Jamie even blurts out his darkest wish in the guise of denying what he assumes Edmund already has guessed: "You suspect right now I'm thinking to myself that Papa is old and can't last much longer, and if you were to die, Mama and I would get all he's got, and so I'm probably hoping—" (163). Edmund *stares at his brother accusingly,* shocked that Jamie indeed may be harboring such thoughts. However, it is not Tyrone's money that Jamie covets so much as the prospect of finally having Mama to himself.

Jamie's feelings seem to repeat those that his mother and father experienced during *their* childhoods. Both Mary and Tyrone adored their opposite-sex parent and viewed their same-sex parent as a rival: even now Tyrone wishes that his father were roasting in hell. The familial pattern descends like a curse through several generations, with disabling results in Jamie. Whereas Mary and Tyrone express milder versions of the parent/child rivalry, Jamie's case is pathological. Indeed, several critics contend that his behavior betrays the symptoms of what Freud diagnosed as the Oedipus complex.[44] According to Freud's theory, a son desires his mother's love and attention to such a degree that he inevitably develops hostility toward his father. However, the son cannot accept such guilty feelings and so represses them. In the normal course of events, according to Freud, the son accedes to his father's power and renounces striving for his mother's exclusive love, taking the father as a model for his future development. In some cases, though, the process fails, leaving the son with unresolved hostility and with sexual attitudes that are confused with childish longings.

Whether or not Freud's theory is a valid model of universal experience, Jamie Tyrone clearly exhibits some of these symptoms. Doubtless, his attitude toward his mother is a tortured one, muddling elements of jealousy and guilt. Moreover, his feelings toward Mary have affected his thinking about women in general. Mary has never forgiven her son for causing her baby's death, and Jamie has never forgiven his mother for violating his ideal of womanhood: "Christ, I'd never dreamed before that any women but whores took dope!" (163).

Jamie's discovery in adolescence of his mother's drug addiction seems to have left him a sexual cripple. He is unable to accept any woman as a marriage partner to fulfill the important role that Mary plays in his life. Instead, he compulsively seeks out prostitutes whom he regards as simultaneously maternal and degrading. The mother/whore dichotomy in Jamie's thinking is so rigid that it sullies his every sexual encounter and so confused that it drives him directly from the cottage to the brothel, leaving no other destination for his love. Why, on the day his mother returns to drugs, does he choose to bury his sorrow in Fat Violet's bosom? Of all the women in Mamie's whorehouse, she is the most maternal. Moreover, like Mary, she plays the piano; like Mary, she has become a burden to those around her; like Mary, she is pitiable and past her prime.[45] Vi seems to appear to Jamie as the unconscious image of his fallen mother, the woman he most longs to possess. The connection is further reinforced when Jamie, returning from the brothel, recites the maudlin refrain from Rudyard Kipling's "Mother O' Mine": "If I were hanged on the highest hill, / Mother o' mine, O mother o' mine! / I know whose love would follow me still . . ." (161). Here, as on other occasions, Jamie vents through the mask of poetry what he cannot express freely in his own voice.

Jamie is regarded by everyone (including himself) as morally unclean, and to his despair he is viewed as a source of pollution spreading contagion throughout the family. His parents think of him as a plague carrier, as the boy who infected his brother with measles and as the man who would like to infect them all with his cynicism. Tyrone openly associates his son with poison. "Beware of that brother of yours," he tells Edmund, "or he'll poison life for you with his damned sneering serpent's tongue!" (109) Jamie's failure in life has "poisoned" his mind, Tyrone thinks (34), and Jamie has tried to poison Edmund's mind ever since the lad was old enough to listen. Mary uses similar imagery, complaining of Jamie's "vile, poisonous tongue" (83). Both parents are intent on isolating Edmund from Jamie, as they are mindful of the past. Of course, the illness now threatening Edmund is not measles but tuberculosis, but they fear that Jamie's continued influence might hasten the course of his disease.

On the symbolic level, the pattern of poison imagery in the play identifies Jamie once again with his mother. Mary is a poisoner, too, in the sense that her addiction threatens to destabilize the family. In Mary's case, however, the toxin is self-administered. Although morphine is rarely mentioned by name in the play, it is referred to throughout as a poison (123, 139, 174). Tyrone excuses Mary's ranting as "the poison talking" (142). "When you have the poison in you," he tells her in act 3, "you want to blame everyone but yourself!" (111). Through this parallel in imagery, O'Neill suggests that Jamie and his mother are the related sources of infection that assail the family unit in *Long Day's Journey into Night*. O'Neill in addition suggests that the only way to cleanse the family is through the process of confession. The climactic speeches in the last act are designed to serve that purpose, absolving the characters from the taint of malicious intent. Jamie's is the most wrenching confession of all; he damns himself in the present whereas the others justify their pasts. This is particularly true of Mary, who cannot account for her present actions by the end of the play. By identifying Jamie and Mary as the family poisoners, O'Neill has Jamie function as a familial scapegoat, scourging his own conscience but also symbolically bearing away the various contagions that plague the Tyrones.

In act 4 Jamie does more than advise Edmund to be on his guard against him. He pronounces his own symbolic death: "Think of me as dead—tell people, 'I had a brother, but he's dead' " (166). Part of Jamie has been dead for a long time, the guilty part that hates life and that perversely has attempted to corrupt Edmund. However, the part of Jamie that is still capable of love now urges him to self-sacrifice. Jamie's warning is one of the most costly gestures of his life, for by cutting Edmund free, he banishes himself from the one person in the world who still accepts him. His warning also is an act of exorcism, for Jamie is still trying to atone for the death he caused as a boy. "Give me credit," he begs Edmund. "Gone to confession. Know you absolve me, don't you, Kid?" (167).

Later, O'Neill decided that Edmund's absolution of Jamie was not enough. After finishing *Long Day's Journey into Night,* he devoted still another play to James Tyrone, Jr., *A Moon for the Misbegotten,* which was to be his last. This play is set eleven years later, in 1923. Now in his early forties, Jamie (he is called "Jim" Tyrone in *A Moon for the Misbegotten*) appears as an alcoholic wreck unable to cope with his mother's recent death. During a long, moonlit night, he pours out his soul to the kind of woman who embodies all his ghosts, Josie Hogan, who also serves as his dead mother's replacement. In *A Moon for the Misbegotten* Josie is a virgin who pretends to be a whore, the reversal of Jamie's image of Mary, who, like a whore, took dope. On the steps of a New England farmhouse, rocked in the arms of this extraordinary woman, who is in turn, virgin, mother, and illusory whore, James Tyrone, Jr., at last finds a measure of peace.

EDMUND TYRONE

In comparison with the other members of the family, Edmund at first appears rather bland. However, that impression is misleading. As the family inheritor, he listens, observes, reflects, and thus serves as the audience's focal point. Perhaps his passivity accounts for the impression that he is the play's least clearly defined character. One critic finds Edmund to be a curiously two-dimensional figure "whose past has been bowdlerized and whose negative characteristics are only lightly touched."[46] Another counters: "Surely Edmund is more than simply the victim of his family, for he has in his own way—through his dissipation, his mistrust of his mother, his academic failures—contributed to the Tyrones' tragedies."[47] The truth lies somewhere between these views. At one point Jamie growls at Edmund: "And it was your being born that started Mama on dope" (166). But of course, Edmund is blameless in this situation, whereas Jamie's disobedience, Mary's addiction, and Tyrone's stinginess are—to some extent, at least—acts of choice. Edmund's birth is not at all his fault, and now the possibility of his death seems to atone for any harm that his life has caused. As far as the others are concerned, Edmund is off the hook.

That is not how Edmund sees it, though. During the play he

expresses a wide range of emotions, including guilt, self-pity, and anger. At times he becomes aggressive. He slaps and punches his brother in act 4 and verbally assaults both parents, calling his mother a dope fiend and his father a stinking miser. As Jamie observes, his brother's quietness fools people into thinking they can manipulate him, but "he's stubborn as hell inside" (35). Like Jamie, Edmund has a sarcastic streak. The stage directions indicate that he grins provocatively, or is sardonic, ironical, or derisive in more than thirty instances. Several aspects of his behavior are depicted in a critical light, particularly his posing and morbidness. *"When he speaks it is as if he were deliberately giving way to drunkenness and seeking to hide behind a maudlin manner"* (152). Sometimes Edmund's sentiments are puerile, such as his remark about life and manure. Here the audience may be inclined to agree with Mary when she accuses Edmund of loving to be dramatic and tragic.

However, these minor flaws in Edmund's personality might be dismissed as tokens of his immaturity (he is only twenty-three years old). His age is one of the important facets of his character. For instance, Edmund has a greater concern for social appearances than he will maintain in later life if he becomes an observant writer. (It galls him to think of his father showing himself up before the whole town as a tightwad.) By the same token, Edmund has the hopefulness of untried youth. Long after the others have given up on Mary, he maintains his optimism. He also demonstrates youth's inconsistency. Although he attacks his father for uselessly preaching "will power" to Mary (141), he takes the same tack himself (92). Earlier in the play he begs his mother to face the truth, but by the end of the play Edmund joins in the family stampede toward repression: "Who wants to see life as it is, if they can help it?" (131).

It is clear what the others are trying to forget, but the details concerning Edmund's personal past are sketchy. O'Neill alludes to a life of romance and adventure and even a suicide attempt, but curiously, these receive less attention than the circumstances surrounding his birth. While in prep school, Edmund began leading a life of dissipation in direct imitation of his brother. Like Jamie, he later was thrown out of college and seems to have ruined his health by leading an irresponsible life. Edmund has "worked his way all over the map as a sailor" and once spent a period on a beach in South America living on rotgut whiskey (35). In the tropics he picked up a touch of malaria, which has weakened his constitution. He has camped on park benches and roomed in filthy dives. Without mentioning specifics, Edmund admits to his father that he has pulled a lot of "rotten stuff" (145). His suicide attempt came when he was living above a bar called Jimmy the Priest's; he almost succeeded. "I was stone cold sober. That was the trouble. I'd stopped to think too long" (147). Now, like Jamie, he has straggled home to spend the summer with the family. One bright note is that Edmund is working for the first time as a cub reporter on the local newspaper, a position that offers him a future. The crucial factor in his life, however, is his illness. Whatever slender hope there is left for the Tyrone family depends on him, but we do not know at the end of the play whether Edmund will live or die.

The plot of *Long Day's Journey into Night* revolves around the interlocking disclosures of Mary's re-addiction and Edmund's consumption. Edmund and his mother are closely linked in other ways, as well. Edmund resembles Mary physically and even shares her nervous temperament. He has her large, dark eyes, hypersensitive mouth, high forehead, and shaky hands. *"It is in the quality of extreme nervous sensibility that the likeness of Edmund to his mother is most marked"* (20). Both have attempted to kill themselves, and both are linked to sanatoriums. Mary has just returned from one, and Edmund will soon leave for one. From Mary, Edmund has learned to love the fog as a means of escape, and from her he has acquired a frightening death wish. Whereas Mary thinks of taking an overdose "by mistake," Edmund longs to become a "ghost within a ghost" (131).

Edmund also has acquired from his mother her gift of imagination. Both have had visionary experiences promising true joy and unity. Mary recalls her "true vision" at the shrine on the little island in the lake when the Virgin smiled and blessed her (175). Edmund has experienced something "like a saint's vision of beatitude" at sea (153). Both are highly emotional, and both have a tendency to stammer.

Mary stammers on five occasions during the play (64, 67, 75, 85, 92). Edmund, too, "*stammers miserably*" when he confronts his mother with his knowledge of her re-addiction (120). Later, when he announces to his father that his purpose in life is to become a writer, he admits that the best he will ever do is stammer—that is, if he lives. "Stammering is the native eloquence of us fog people" (154). In the manuscript for *Long Day's Journey into Night,* O'Neill originally used the word "stuttering." In the first typewritten draft, he carefully crossed out "stuttering" and changed it to "stammering," as if to reinforce the connection between Edmund's voice and his mother's.[48] By linking Mary to Edmund in this way, O'Neill suggests a hopeful message. If her son lives, Mary's visionary impulse, so poorly expressed during her own life in unrealistic dreams, may find through Edmund a true destination in art.

But before that can happen, Edmund must escape his mother's influence. One critic suggests that "Edmund's struggle to separate from his mother . . . is the very spine of the play."[49] With the example before us of Jamie's failure to do so, it is clear that for Edmund the stakes in this struggle are high. Throughout the play Mary tries to manipulate him with "*bullying motherliness*" (120), and in her presence Edmund slips into an immature posture, often sounding like a hurt child. There are four important scenes between Mary and Edmund, and in each Edmund feels powerless to shape the interaction. In the third act he finally explodes: "Listen, Mama. I'm going to tell you whether you want to hear it or not. I've got to go to a sanatorium" (119). When Mary still refuses to hear what Edmund is trying to tell her, he unleashes his pent-up anger and calls her a "dope fiend" (120). Then he breaks down. In their last encounter in act 4, Edmund pathetically breaks down again. He tugs at his mother's arm to claim her attention: "Mama! It isn't a summer cold! I've got consumption!" In the stage directions O'Neill comments: "*As he pleads he has the quality of a bewilderedly hurt little boy*" (174).

Edmund's other psychological challenge in the play is to evade the influence of Jamie.[50] Indeed, Edmund always has looked to his older brother as a model. (Models are important to the Tyrones. Mary has

Mother Elizabeth; Tyrone has Edwin Booth. That Jamie himself has no one to look up to is part of his tragedy.) Jamie insists that he has had more to do with Edmund's upbringing than anyone else. "I made you! You're my Frankenstein!" he asserts (164). But Jamie also poses the most significant danger to Edmund. Jamie has shaped Edmund's attitudes toward sex, alcohol, and even literature: "And because I wanted once to write, I planted it in your mind that someday you'd write!" (164). Recognizing the inevitability of his own failure, Jamie has lived vicariously through Edmund. The crucial question is, to what extent has Edmund come to see the world through Jamie's eyes?

At the end of *Long Day's Journey into Night* the residue of Jamie's tutelage still clings to Edmund. He is sick, drunk, and unattached, like his older brother. As far as can be gathered, Edmund has had no relationships with any women other than prostitutes, again like Jamie. We know that Edmund is a visitor to Mamie Burns's place, because when Jamie informs him that he picked Fat Violet, Edmund knows exactly whom he means: "Some pick! God, she weighs a ton" (159). Several of Edmund's favorite metaphors are drawn from his acquaintance with prostitutes: he compares the dripping fog to "the dreary tears of a trollop spattering in a puddle of stale beer on a honky-tonk table top!" (152). In perhaps an unconscious transition, Edmund moves directly from this memory to recounting the "high spots" of his life. His key monologue about the sea begins through this associative process and pivots on a phrase that has the double meaning of "streetwalker" and "sailing vessel": "The old hooker driving fourteen knots . . ." (153). Originally, a "hooker" designated a one-masted sailing boat; later it became a contemptuous term for a clumsy old craft, and in another shift, sailors' slang for prostitute.

Edmund and Jamie have shared similar sordid experiences. But whereas Jamie flees to prostitutes to blot out his dreams of Mary, Edmund has begun to sublimate his desire to "belong" by identifying his quest for unity with the sea. What Broadway is for Jamie, the ocean is for Edmund. Later he will seek fulfillment through his art. While it may be too late for Jamie to undo the cluster of associations that degrades his relationships with women, Edmund's poetic sensibility offers him an avenue of escape, and Jamie realizes this as he urges his brother to cast him aside. O'Neill suggests that Edmund already has begun moving away from Jamie by a subtle contrast between the brothers toward the end of the play. Jamie, drunk, stumbles over the steps in the fog, just as Edmund declares that if he ever becomes a writer, he will "stammer" on behalf of all "fog people" (154). Jamie's stumbling is another stage in his decline, but Edmund's stammering is a sign of hope. If Edmund lives, he will speak for his brother, too.

By the final act, Edmund has begun the painful process of separating from both his mother and his brother. Simultaneously, he begins drawing closer to his father, as if fulfilling a necessary stage in his progression toward adulthood. Edmund's redefinition of his relationship to Tyrone is one of the important developments in *Long Day's Journey into Night*. Their reconciliation begins after a violent argument during which Edmund takes his mother's part and rehashes all her grievances against Tyrone. His father objects: "Will you stop repeating your mother's crazy accusations?" (142). The precise moment when the tide begins to change is when Tyrone speaks feelingly about his own mother. At the beginning of Tyrone's monologue, Edmund listens rather passively, but he becomes fully absorbed when James describes his mother's suffering. For the first time Edmund is visibly "*moved*," and he joins in with an assenting comment (148). For Edmund to begin thinking of his father as a son is new and significant, and from this point on, he is able to empathize with Tyrone, experiencing the past, for a change, through his father's eyes.

Once Edmund begins to identify with his father, he is riveted by Tyrone's tale of talent squandered and ambition lost. As Edmund listens, he silently resolves to learn from his father's negative example and to devote himself faithfully to his own budding talent. In response to his father's shared intimacy, Edmund launches into his monologue on the sea, inviting his father to judge his fledging effort as a wordsmith. When he has finished, Tyrone stares at him, impressed. "There's the makings of a poet in you, all right," he tells his son (154). Encouraged, Edmund pronounces his artistic credo. If he does live to be a poet, he will strive for "faithful realism," but beyond the surface

The original Broadway cast. From left to right: Florence Eldridge as Mary, Bradford Dillman as Edmund, Jason Robards, Jr., as Jamie, Fredric March as James Tyrone. Photograph courtesy of the Collection of American Literature, Beinecke Rare Book and Manuscript Library, Yale University.

of his words will hover an unattainable ideal that realism cannot represent, a glimpse of unity, or "belonging." That quality seems painfully absent in the lives of the Tyrones, and it is the goal toward which Edmund's art aspires: "For a second you see—and seeing the secret, are the secret. For a second there is meaning!" (153).

But even if Edmund lives to become the fine artist that his father might have been, he will bear the scars of his family history. His father's failure, his brother's anguish, and his mother's addiction will corrode his instinct for happiness, and the tragedy of his guilt-ridden birth will haunt him forever. In his own estimation, Edmund will always remain "a stranger who never feels at home, who does not really want and is not really wanted, who can never belong, who must always be a little in love with death!" (153–54).

The Four Haunted Tyrones

Is it possible to say which of the four major characters is the central figure in the play? O'Neill, it seems, divides the multiple functions of the traditional hero among his principals. As he suggests in his dedication, *Long Day's Journey into Night* belongs to "*all* the four haunted Tyrones." Each member of the family supports the canopy of collective guilt on the pole of a personal injury. Each has a separate voice, yet together they form a tragic chorus. As the curtain falls, Mary, Tyrone, Jamie, and Edmund are united in their suffering. Whose play is it, then? The family as a whole is the protagonist of *Long Day's Journey into Night*.

DRAMATIC LANGUAGE: "THE MAKINGS OF A POET"

7

The *makings* of a poet. No, I'm afraid I'm like the guy who is always panhandling for a smoke. He hasn't even got the makings. He's only got the habit.

—Edmund, *Long Day's Journey into Night,* act 4

O'NEILL'S DRAMATIC LANGUAGE

The art of *Long Day's Journey into Night* lies in O'Neill's mastery of language as well as in the complex psychology of his characters. To fully appreciate the play, a reader must attend to the special quality of its dialogue, remembering that in the theater the spoken and not the written word serves as the medium of exchange. All through his career O'Neill was haunted by the difficulty of creating a dramatic language suitable to his talents. On the one hand, he believed that "faithful realism" (Edmund's phrase) was a desirable necessity. In an age of prose, audiences could not be expected to respond to verse or elevated diction as had Shakespeare's spectators at the Globe. Besides, such language was beyond his range. Yet any attempt at realism that was

68

slavishly faithful to everyday speech would, he felt, result in an instrument too blunt to convey psychological truths. Every modern playwright confronts this paradox. The problem is how to avoid stilted "literary" language while also eschewing the vagaries of mere conversation. Perhaps O'Neill felt the pangs of this dilemma more keenly than most of his contemporaries. His true subjects in the theater, he announced, were the "inscrutable forces behind life which it is my intention to shadow at their work in my plays."[51] The "realism" toward which O'Neill strove declared its fidelity to these deeper currents of human conflict and not the superficial eddies of the quotidian; yet how might a writer express life's inscrutable forces without recourse to poetic means?

In *Long Day's Journey into Night* O'Neill describes his own frustrations through Edmund's self-deprecatory remarks to his father. Does Edmund truly have the makings of a poet? Alas, no, he replies, he has only the yearning but lacks the innate poetic gift. Acknowledging this handicap, Edmund will struggle to become an artist by relying on his talent for realism. O'Neill was speaking of himself. Throughout most of his career critics complained that his dramatic language fell below the level of his characters, and he generally conceded the point. In his personal correspondence O'Neill frequently complained of his inability to phrase memorable speeches. In one letter to Arthur Hobson Quinn, he confessed simply: *Mourning Becomes Electra* "needed great language to lift it beyond itself. I haven't got that. And by way of self-consolation, I don't think . . . that great language is possible for anyone living in the discordant, broken, faithless rhythm of our time."[52] As if to compensate for his uneasiness with dramatic language, O'Neill devoted much of his energy in his early years to a number of stylistic experiments, using dialects, interior monologues, masks, music, and other stage effects to convey emotion. His ability to visualize a scene on stage gave rise to his most successful techniques. O'Neill triumphed with such devices as the scenic conceptualization of a symbolic forest in *The Emperor Jones,* a society girl's descent into the stokehole of an ocean liner in *The Hairy Ape,* contracting walls and ceilings in *All God's Chillun Got Wings,* a cut-away farmhouse in

Desire under the Elms, and the ballet of masks in *The Great God Brown.* Yet his failure to compose intensely moving dialogue continued to gnaw at him: "Masks in that connection demand great language to speak—which let me out with a sickening bump!"[53]

Paradoxically, it was during O'Neill's self-imposed exile in California, during the silent years when no new plays of his were mounted, that he began to feel his way at last toward a mature, flexible, and naturally dignified prose style. O'Neill drew directly on his own experience without interposing, as he had in the 1920s, screens of allegory and symbolism to separate his memories from his art. Perhaps his recollection of the lilting Irish-American speech that he had learned at home provided the opening he needed. O'Neill does not exploit the stereotypical brogue of the stage Irishman in *Long Day's Journey into Night.*[54] Rather, he draws on the resources available to him for portraying speakers of standard American English who just happen to be graced with poetic rhythm and a capacity for fiery outbursts. In *Long Day's Journey into Night,* the result is O'Neill's finest achievement in dramatic dialogue.

The Tyrones' speech patterns have the admirable ring of naturalness that any credo of realism might demand. The family members speak precisely and yet easily, their moods modifying their syntax. When they are angry, the flavor of their heated argument is rendered forcefully. When they relent, their words soften and their syllables linger. The play's speeches consistently reveal character, define relationships, provide background information, further the plot, highlight key issues, and focus the dramatic moment. But in addition to performing these basic functions of realistic dialogue, O'Neill's dramatic language for the first time extends its range to include any number of memorable lines, among them: "None of us can help the things life has done to us" (61); "Then Mother of God, why do I feel so lonely?" (95); "I would have been much more successful as a seagull or a fish" (150). In *Long Day's Journey into Night* the makings of a poet surface at last.

O'Neill gives each character a distinctive, personalized voice. As long as she is in control of herself, Mary has a fine command of phrasing, but as time goes on, we hear the insecure tones of a defensive woman who increasingly withdraws and evades issues. In the end she regresses to the immature speech patterns of a stammering schoolgirl. She remembers only that "something happened" to her, falling into the passive voice, which becomes her signature key. By contrast, Tyrone relies on the stentorian tones of the accomplished actor, but toward evening his voice is tinged with guilt and shame. Jamie is noted for his sarcasm and Broadway lingo, which he uses to disguise his feelings. Edmund's voice is more tentative, except when he waxes poetical or imitates his brother's slang. Midway through the play all the characters begin to express themselves more honestly. Tyrone and Mary accept the ugly epithets of "miser" and "dope fiend," Edmund allows his childishness to show, and Jamie drops his devil-may-care pose.

The major characters are most sharply defined during their extended speeches of act 4. Each of the soliloquies begins with a concrete anecdote and then builds toward a climactic moment of personal triumph through the swelling of narrative rhythm. In each case the moment of ascendancy proves ephemeral and is framed by an abrupt readjustment downward. A structural analysis of the respective monologues of Tyrone, Edmund, and Mary clearly reveals this pattern:

	Anecdote	*Triumph*	*Decline*
TYRONE:	"It was at home I first learned the value of a dollar."	"I had life where I wanted it."	". . . and then life had me where it wanted me."
EDMUND:	"I lay on the bowsprit facing astern."	"Then the moment of ecstatic freedom came."	"Then the hand lets the veil fall."
MARY:	"I had a talk with Mother Elizabeth."	"I knew . . . that the Blessed Virgin had smiled and blessed me."	"Then in the spring something happened to me."

For each of the Tyrones, the past intervenes between the remembered peak experience and the present. The form each monologue takes imitates the natural rhythm of the life cycle, progressing from youth to maturation to decline. Each monologue enacts in miniature the dramatic rhythm of the play, which moves from day to night and, by implication, from life toward death.

Although similar in structure, the monologues achieve their impact through stylistic methods appropriate to the character speaking. Tyrone's remembrance builds upon a catalog of sorrows in progressive, serial order, each strengthening his overall defense: he describes his siblings, the machine shop, what it was like for the family at Christmas, etc. Mary's closing speech depends for its effect on her sad confusion of past and present time frames. Edmund's description of his sea voyages is the most self-consciously crafted of the monologues, and the most static and abstract in syntax and diction. Its subject, the intangible experience of feeling mystically at one with nature, is more difficult to convey than either Tyrone's poverty or Mary's convent memories. The key to its delivery lies in its dramatic context, which is the growing intimacy that it signals between Edmund and Tyrone.

Technically, Jamie's drunken confession to his brother, in contrast to the three soliloquies in act 4, is structured as a dialogue. The playwright must have concluded that the fourth act could not support another monologue following so closely on the heels of Tyrone's and Edmund's. Even so, Edmund barely interrupts, and the stage is given over to Jamie. His rambling speech inverts the pattern of the other monologues by stressing the present rather than the past. Propelled by self-disgust, not reminiscence, Jamie is hoping to change the direction of Edmund's life. Although he has no moment of past triumph to describe, he does achieve a victory of sorts when he finally feels cleansed and worthy for the first time of his brother's trust.

In terms of dramatic rhythm, Jamie's Fat Violet anecdote sharply alters the pace of the act, coming as it does after Edmund's romantic soliloquizing. The contrast is intentional, for O'Neill carefully planned the four extended speeches in the last act to vary in mood and tone. Tyrone's highly dramatic life story is first, followed by Edmund's languorous ode to the sea. Next, to quicken the pace, comes Jamie's highly charged confession. Mary's softer, elegiacal monologue, which repeats the rhythm of Edmund's soliloquy, brings the play to a close.

Dramatic Language

The Web of Literary Allusions

An unusual feature of *Long Day's Journey into Night* is O'Neill's frequent use of literary quotations. Sometimes he introduces entire stanzas of other poets' work. Directors often are tempted to cut these from performance, but the verse units are integral to the dialogue. Not only do they function to define characters and their relationships, they also contribute to the play's emotional impact. The Tyrones are a highly literate as well as a theatrical family. Edmund is an avid reader, and both Tyrone and Jamie have had to memorize lines for the stage, so O'Neill has a natural explanation for the presence of quotations. He can freely intersperse poetry and prose without violating the tenets of realism.

A fine example is Jamie's recitation from Algernon Swinburne's "A Leave-Taking," which expresses the collective emotion of the men as Mary withdraws at the conclusion of the play.

> Let us go hence, my songs; she will not hear.
> Let us go hence together without fear;
> Keep silence now, for singing-time is over,
> And over all old things and all things dear.
> She loves not you nor me as we all love her.
> Yea, though we sang as angels in her ear,
> She would not hear.[55]

Swinburne's text lights up the moment like a verbal spotlight. The passage lends weight and dignity to Jamie's response ("Keep silence now, for singing-time is over"), fixes the image of Mary's oblivion ("She would not hear"), and etches the Tyrones' pain ("She loves not you nor me as we all love her"). The cadences of the verse intensify the emotion projected to the audience and help move the play toward closure. (Only in the last act are longer passages of poetry recited.) Through this process O'Neill can summon poets from the past to function as a chorus in what remains a rigorously modern play.

O'Neill carefully planned to include these passages. Among his early handwritten notes for the play is a page containing a list of verse quotations for act 4.[56] On the list are five selections for Jamie and one for Tyrone. Jamie's quotations include lines from Rudyard Kipling's "Ford O' Kabul River," as well as his "Sestina of the Tramp-Royal" and "Mother O' Mine"; Dante Gabriel Rossetti's Sonnet XLVI from *House of Life* ("Look in my face; my name is Might-have-been"); and Shakespeare's speech from *Richard III* that begins "Clarence is come." The other Shakespearean reference on the sheet is Tyrone's important quotation from *Julius Caesar,* "The fault, dear Brutus, is not in our stars, / But in ourselves . . ." (140–41). O'Neill obviously planned to use this speech but seemed unsure of its final placement. The quotation is inserted with a caret in act 4 of the pencil manuscript, suggesting that the speech was added after the first draft was complete. Edmund's "days of wine and roses" quotation from Ernest Dowson similarly was added with a caret, and so was Jamie's "Mother O' Mine" speech.

While the quotations in *Long Day's Journey into Night* enrich the play's linguistic medium, they also serve to better define the characters. When pressed, Tyrone falls back upon Shakespeare, Edmund and Jamie cite their contemporary favorites, and Mary relies on her Catholic religious tradition (in act 3 she recites the Hail Mary, and in act 4 she quotes Mother Elizabeth as an authority).

Tyrone's Shakespearean references generally fall into two categories. He uses Shakespeare either to dramatize his emotions ("How sharper than a serpent's tooth it is / To have a thankless child!") or to lecture his sons ("The fault, dear Brutus . . ."). Tyrone draws upon a limited range of Shakespeare's plays (*King Lear, The Tempest, Julius Caesar,* and *As You Like It*). His quotations, not always accurate, remind us of his failure to pursue a classical career.[57] His sons tend to use Shakespeare to antagonize him. Once Edmund won a wager from Tyrone by memorizing Macbeth's part in a week. Now he butchers the bard: "We are such stuff as manure is made on, so let's drink up and forget it" (131). Jamie similarly mocks his father by reciting from *Othello* to ridicule Tyrone's snoring, or by quoting *Hamlet* with a sneer to dramatize Mary's entrance: "The Mad Scene. Enter Ophelia!" (170). In response, Edmund slaps Jamie across the mouth and wins his father's praise for the rebuke.

Dramatic Language

The play's literary allusions help delineate relationships in the family. Tyrone, for example, refuses to enter into a literary debate with Jamie but is eager to do so with Edmund. Edmund advances the claims of his turn-of-the-century favorites, but Tyrone counters stubbornly that Shakespeare said it all and said it better. More important than the content is the passionate tone of this argument. Here father and son communicate on a topic of mutual interest; what begins as an impersonal discussion provides a platform for their growing intimacy. Moreover, the audience learns a good deal about Tyrone and Edmund during their exchange. Tyrone accuses Edmund of morbidness based on his taste in authors; he himself counsels resignation, using Shakespeare as his guide. Tyrone's taste and philosophy are informed by age, whereas Edmund's literary taste signals his youthful need to break with the past.

The poets Edmund champions (Swinburne, Symons, Baudelaire, Dowson, Wilde, Rossetti) are linked to the turn-of-the-century literary movement known as Decadence (Symons proposed the term in a manifesto published in 1893). The Decadents heralded the decay of nineteenth-century optimism and faith, proclaiming themselves to be the vanguard of revolutionary ideas. In revolt against prudishness, they sought to modernize poetry by choosing such subjects as drugs and alcohol, illicit sex, and the seamy underside of city life. Freethinking, uninhibited (though verbally decorous), these aesthetes cultivated a pose of studied perversity, praising the forbidden and eulogizing fleeting moments of intense feeling. Their credo scandalized the older generation, so (naturally) the Decadents would have been irresistibly appealing to a writer of Edmund's age. But Edmund's attraction to the group also signifies less than a full-blown philosophy. No doubt he will shed the skin of his teenage reading as he develops a writer's voice of his own; for now it is enough that he seeks to explore the literature of his own time.

Edmund has adopted uncritically his brother's taste in literature. Jamie is the most prolific quoter of verse in *Long Day's Journey into Night*, citing late nineteenth-century poets on seven occasions in act 4 alone. (In addition, Jamie cites Shakespeare three times in act 4, the

Bible once, and he also alludes to a play and a novel.) Whereas Edmund quotes to validate his views, Jamie's literary allusions serve a variety of functions. Jamie quotes to mock ("Clarence is come"), to express self-pity ("If I were hanged on the highest hill"), indifference ("Speakin' in general, I 'ave tried 'em all"), or cynicism ("Therefore put money in thy purse"). He quotes also to find company in his sordid behavior, reciting from Wilde's "The Harlot's House" on his return from the brothel. Some of Jamie's quotations contain significant clues to his character, a notable instance being his recasting of lines from "The Ballad of Reading Gaol." Wilde's original lines are: "The man had killed the thing he loved / And so he had to die."[58] According to Jamie, Wilde got the meaning twisted: "The man was dead and so he had to kill the thing he loved. That's what it ought to be" (166). Because Jamie is dead inside, he seems to be saying, he has tried to destroy Edmund, the brother whom he loves. The reference takes on additional meaning for the reader who knows that in a later verse Wilde specifically alludes to Cain's murder of Abel and "How men their brothers maim."[59]

According to Edmund, Jamie's favorite quotation is a stanza from Ernest Dowson's "Cynara," a contemporary poem in which the speaker in mock cynicism asserts that he has been faithful to his absent lover, Cynara, even while lying in the arms of a prostitute.

> Surely the kisses of her bought red mouth were sweet;
> But I was desolate and sick of an old passion,
> When I awoke and found the dawn was gray:
> I have been faithful to thee, Cynara! in my fashion.[60]

Edmund adds the comment that Jamie "never loved any Cynara, and was never faithful to a woman in his life, even in his fashion!" (134). Several critics have remarked that if there were ever a Cynara in Jamie's life, it could only have been his mother.[61] In this case Jamie uses quotation to express the forbidden contents of his unconscious mind.

Finally, O'Neill employs literary allusions in the play to heighten dramatic parallels. Jamie's influence over Edmund is suggested through the literary allusions that they share. It is Edmund, pointedly, who recites Jamie's favorite Dowson poem. Edmund also quotes from Baudelaire's cynical poem "Epilogue" and remarks that it conjures "a good likeness of Jamie . . . hiding in a Broadway hotel room with some fat tart" (134). When Jamie later relates his encounter with Fat Violet, Edmund quotes from the poem again, this time more in a tone of conspiratorial camaraderie, suggesting that he shares some of his brother's attitudes (160).

The web of literary allusions in *Long Day's Journey into Night* is pulled tight when Edmund consciously takes note of the parallel between himself and Dowson: "Poor Dowson. Booze and consumption got him" (135). Quickly he volunteers to change the subject. Tyrone falls into the same pattern, condemning Edmund's favorite writers as "whoremongers and degenerates," which brings to mind Jamie. Edmund counters that Shakespeare was "a souse," which in turn reflects on Tyrone's present condition. Tyrone completes the irony by blurting out that Rossetti was a "dope fiend" (135). Unwittingly and much to his chagrin, Tyrone thereby completes the family album.

POETRY OF THE THEATER

In addition to poetry *in* the theater, that is to say, language dependent on the spoken word, O'Neill fully exploits the poetry *of* the theater, using a variety of nonverbal techniques to express meaning and emotion. Such devices include gestures, blocking (the physical movement of actors on stage), sound and lighting effects, and other scenic images. What passes in the text as an offhand stage direction can become a telling event in the theater: witness the moment in act 2 when Tyrone absorbs the knowledge of Mary's relapse with a silent stare, or the final tableau when the men *"slowly lower their drinks to the table, forgetting them"* (175).

Throughout *Long Day's Journey into Night* significant gestures and groupings punctuate the characters' speeches. The opening of act

2, scene 2, builds upon a purely visual tension as the Tyrones isolate Mary, avoiding touching or looking at her. Mary faces front like an accused criminal, one hand fumbling with the bosom of her dress, the other drumming nervously on the tabletop. James lights a cigar and goes to the screen door, looking out. Jamie lights a pipe and moves to the window. Edmund drops into a chair and turns away. The situation is immediately comprehensible. As the scene continues, the effects of Mary's altered state are conveyed through her gestures as well as her words.

O'Neill masterfully uses sound and lighting effects to define the play's motifs. The melancholy foghorn and the warning bells on yachts anchored in the harbor sound at measured intervals; the telephone in act 2 and Mary's piano playing in act 4 are startling interruptions of mood. O'Neill most effectively combines visual and auditory techniques in the middle of act 3 to mark the transition from Mary's scene with Cathleen to her reception of the returning men. As the room darkens perceptibly, the moan of the foghorn is heard *"followed by a chorus of bells, muffled by the fog"* (107). Mary has been staring fixedly. Now she attempts to pray, and at the sound of the men coming up the front path she springs up. An instant later the front-hall light comes on and shines through the parlor, bathing her in light. Mary is simultaneously glad and unhappy that the men have returned. The lighting change carries this message, rescuing Mary from the dark but at the same time betraying her hiding place.

The play's most memorable example of symbolic lighting occurs in the last act when Tyrone gropes for the bulbs in the chandelier. As he reaches the end of his confession to Edmund, he cannot bear his own revelations.

No, I don't know what the hell it was that I wanted to buy. *He clicks out one bulb.* On my solemn oath, Edmund, I'd gladly face not having an acre of land to call my own, nor a penny in the bank—*He clicks out another bulb.* I'd be willing to have no home but the poorhouse in my old age if I could look back now on having been the fine artist I might have been. *He turns out a third bulb, so only*

*the reading lamp is on, and sits down again heavily. Edmund sud-
denly cannot hold back a burst of strained, ironical laughter.* (151)

The moment is quintessentially theatrical. Not only does Tyrone vividly demonstrate his incorrigibility as a miser, but symbolically he
shows himself to be a proponent of the dark. He literally dims the
stage, reminding the audience of his central role in the family's
nightward journey.

In such theatrical moments, O'Neill's artistry as a stage poet is
never in doubt. Yet that alone failed to satisfy him. "Where I feel
myself most neglected," he once wrote, diverging from his usual self-
criticism, "is just where I set most store by myself—as a bit of a poet,
who has labored with the spoken word to evolve original rhythms of
beauty, where beauty apparently isn't" (*Selected Letters,* 195). "A bit
of a poet," "the makings of a poet"—O'Neill evidently was beguiled
by the permutations of this phrase; he even called another of his plays
"A Touch of the Poet." Throughout his career O'Neill evaluated his
talent modestly. As a playwright he won the world's respect, yet critics
still are reluctant to praise him as a writer. Considering his mastery of
both spoken and nonspoken language in *Long Day's Journey into
Night,* perhaps it is time to grant O'Neill the title he coveted most.

THE PLAY AS TRAGEDY
8

None of us can help the things life has done to us.
—Mary, *Long Day's Journey into Night,* act 2

Examining the setting, dramatic structure, characters, and language of *Long Day's Journey into Night* provides a context in which to consider in broader terms the vision of life that emerges in the play. What, after all, is the purpose of depicting human suffering in tragedy? Has that aim changed over time in Western culture, and if so, with what result? O'Neill's thinking on tragedy evolved significantly during the course of his career, and in order to clarify his position, it is necessary to begin at his point of entry into a debate that really began with Aristotle.

ARISTOTLE ON TRAGEDY

As the first theoretician of tragedy, Aristotle has had an enormous influence in shaping our views on the subject. His ideas about the tragic hero, tragic error, tragic action, and recognition have become obligatory points of discussion in subsequent criticism. O'Neill possessed a well-marked copy of the *Poetics,* but he tended to dispute Aristotle's authority, especially on the issue of catharsis, which forms the cornerstone of the Greek philosopher's theory. In the *Poetics,* Aristotle argues that the ultimate purpose of tragedy is to excite pity and fear in the spectator so as to "purge" or "purify" these emotions. (Literally translated from the Greek, catharsis means "purgation.") What Aristotle precisely means by fear and pity is unclear, nor does he explain in any detail why purging those emotions is desirable.

However, he argues that in order for the tragic effect to occur, certain conditions must be met, especially in the characterization of the hero. First, the hero must be of sufficient stature and nobility to invite our admiration. Second, he cannot be perceived as truly evil or his punishment will seem all too deserving; in that case no spectator could feel pity. On the other hand, the protagonist cannot be perceived as truly innocent, for then a spectator would be unable to recoil in terror from his deeds. For Aristotle, this ambivalent response of attraction and repulsion is a necessary precondition for experiencing catharsis. "There remains, then, the character between these two extremes—that of a man who is not eminently good and just, yet whose misfortune is brought about not by vice or depravity, but by some error or frailty."[62] He stresses that the hero is a moral agent, a person of superior mental gifts but only average morality who unwittingly engineers his own defeat. Fate may play a part, but ethical action is the key. Thus the hero must be shown choosing or avoiding the good.

These prescriptions may seem transparent, but Aristotle leaves a great deal open to interpretation. For example, does Aristotle's term for "error" (hamartia in Greek; literally, "missing the mark") mean what we today think of as a sin, a mistake, or a tragic flaw? Each of these terms is subtly different. Many other questions arise. Does it matter whether the hero's error is intentional or inadvertent? How can someone choose the good if he is ignorant? What is the good? Must we believe in moral absolutes in order to be receptive to tragedy? And what does Aristotle mean by significant stature as a criterion for heroism? Might not the misfortunes of average citizens with no special gifts or elevated social position elicit the desired tragic response? On these issues Aristotle sheds little light. He does insist that the actions imitated in tragedy are appropriate only if they are conducive to purging pity and fear.

The debate over interpreting Aristotle was already overripe by O'Neill's day. "As for Aristotle's 'purging,' " O'Neill comments in a letter, "I think it is about time we purged his purging out of modern criticism." He continues:

> What we need is a definition of Modern and Classical Tragedy by which to guide our judgments. If we had Gods or a God, if we had a faith, if we had some healing subterfuge by which to conquer Death, then the Aristotelian criterion might apply in part to our Tragedy. But our tragedy is just that we have only ourselves, that there is nothing to be purged into except a belief in the guts of man, good or evil, who faces unflinchingly the black mystery of his own soul! (*Selected Letters*, 390)

O'Neill's reading of Aristotle suggests that the spectator of tragedy must be purged "into" something, presumably a desirable emotional condition or belief. No one knows whether Aristotle intended such a reading; purging might simply mean "getting rid of" troublesome emotions. But for O'Neill, the goal of tragedy is to widen the spectator's awareness and sympathies, and here he expresses his frustration as a modern playwright who feels deprived of a clear faith to undergird his mission.

ZOLA AND NIETZSCHE

O'Neill's comments echo the bitter disillusionment that seized many of his generation. For some who came of age at the turn of the century it seemed that the old pieties of the True, the Beautiful, and the Good had been replaced by Capital (Marx), Sex (Freud), and Evolution (Darwin) as the unromantic explanations of the forces driving human history. A new doctrine known as naturalism arose in fiction and the drama, spearheaded by the French novelist and playwright Émile Zola ("Your dirty Zola," Tyrone calls him in the play when castigating Edmund's reading habits). According to Zola, the arts ought to acknowledge the triumph of the only system of thought that had not been undermined, namely Science. On stage, humankind should be redefined as the product of purely "natural" forces, such as heredity and environment. Material conditions governed choice; spiritual freedom was an illusion.

As a youth, O'Neill was susceptible to Zola's influence, but he never completely embraced the naturalists' creed. He realized that the doctrine of naturalism, like the *Poetics*, held profound implications for the theater. However, naturalism lent itself most easily to the drama of social protest, for which O'Neill felt himself temperamentally unsuited. In most social protest plays the central characters are conceived as passive victims of heredity, environment, prejudice, economic deprivation, or misguided social policy. They are fundamentally powerless and, therefore, ultimately not responsible for their suffering. Such figures can spark pity and outrage at injustice, but they are not tragic, at least not in Aristotle's specific sense. For how can such characters choose or avoid the good, if others already have chosen for them? O'Neill's political sympathies generally were with the downtrodden, but his talent did not lie in the direction of the protest play.

After wrestling with his dilemma, O'Neill turned toward the explanation of tragedy found in the theoretical writings of Friedrich Nietzsche, who rejects naturalism as well as Aristotle. Nietzsche specifically rejects a moralistic discussion of tragedy by tracing Greek drama to its origins in ritualistic frenzy. But like Aristotle, Nietzsche argues that the key to understanding tragedy lies in its emotional effect upon the spectator. Nietzsche observes in *The Birth of Tragedy* that the theater has the power to sweep us up in the tow of extraordinary personalities. He mentions such great tragic heroes of the past as Oedipus and Prometheus who, he argues, challenge our very assumptions about individuality. The "errors" of these towering individuals are their egos; both their grandeur and their failure stem from the same source—their illusion of omnipotent selfhood.

The shattering of the hero's illusion invokes Dionysus, who symbolizes humanity's collective instinct to "belong." According to Nietzsche, the Greek tragic chorus, which guides the spectator toward fellow feeling with the suffering hero, expresses the unity of emotion the early Greeks associated with Dionysus. But Nietzsche contends that the tragic implies no higher reality or system of ethical belief. The hero's fate symbolizes the natural rhythm of life; for Nietzsche, the spectator's glimpse of this Dionysian truth is the very aim of tragedy.

In this formulation O'Neill found a satisfying explanation for what the spectator might be purged "into": an acceptance of the life-impulse as a sustaining force.

> And just here is where I am a most confirmed mystic, too, for I'm always, always trying to interpret Life in terms of lives, never just lives in terms of character. I'm always acutely conscious of the Force behind—(Fate, God, our biological past creating our present, whatever one calls it—Mystery, certainly)—and of the one eternal tragedy of Man in his glorious, self-destructive struggle to make the Force express him instead of being, as an animal is, an infinitesimal incident in its expression. (*Selected Letters*, 195)

This statement by O'Neill, written in the 1920s, is extraordinary in its latitude. Are we subject to fate? Perhaps. Are we liable to be held accountable for our choices by a superior moral being? Perhaps. Or, are we driven by heredity and environment, as the naturalists claim? These various philosophies, O'Neill implies (by lumping them together dismissively between parentheses) are just so many interpretations. Only one truth is clear: life is a compelling mystery, and when man in his arrogance attempts to dominate that mystery, or to insist that he personally is at the center of the universe, disaster is likely to ensue.

Although Nietzschean in tone, O'Neill's formulation of tragedy also borrows from Aristotle. It pictures the hero as a moral agent who ignores life's underlying realities and who consequently must be held accountable for his own self-destruction. Applying this theory in his plays of the 1920s, O'Neill implicitly or explicitly condemns his characters for their moral failings. In such works as *The Emperor Jones*,

The Play as Tragedy

Diff'rent, The Hairy Ape, The Fountain, Welded, All God's Chillun Got Wings, Desire under the Elms, Marco Millions, The Great God Brown, and *Mourning Becomes Electra,* retribution defines the action. O'Neill's moral posture in these early plays derives not from stern Puritanism, which he continually attacked, but rather from his reading of Nietzsche and Aristotle and his study of classical tragedy, where error leads to reversal, and pity for the sufferer is tempered by terror at his deeds.

O'NEILL'S SYNTHESIS

As he grew older, O'Neill continued to modify his views on guilt and moral responsibility. His description of *The Iceman Cometh* expresses his mature attitude: "There are moments in it that suddenly strip the secret soul of a man stark naked, not in cruelty or moral superiority, but with an understanding compassion which sees him as a victim of the ironies of life and of himself" (*Selected Letters,* 511). At last O'Neill synthesizes the views of Nietzsche, Zola, and Aristotle into one uniquely his own. On the one hand, life is the victimizer; on the other, we victimize ourselves. Not only does biology impel us to assert our egos, but each of us is conditioned by circumstance and experience to choose or avoid the good in a predictable way. In that sense, a person's past can become his fate. To what extent, then, are we still responsible for our choices? That issue, O'Neill concluded, is undecidable. He did not reverse himself on the question of human culpability; rather, he finally stopped trying to answer it.

O'Neill's emphasis in the later plays shifts from a concern with attributing guilt to a concern with absolving it. Reflecting this change, the terms "compassion," "pity," and "forgiveness" appear with greater frequency in his later writing. We can glimpse this new attitude through Edmund's voice in act 4 of *Long Day's Journey into Night.* "What the devil are you laughing at?" Tyrone demands, after he has completed his confessional monologue. "Not at you, Papa," Edmund replies. "At life. It's so damned crazy" (151).

In keeping with his mature stance, O'Neill does not pinpoint blame in the Tyrone family. Who ultimately is responsible for the suffering in their lives? Mary? Tyrone? Tyrone's father? The hotel doctor? Where does the chain of guilt end, and where does it begin? Throughout the day the Tyrones trade charges incessantly, and then withdraw them. Tyrone complains that Mary blames everyone but herself but then concedes "she's not responsible" (139). Jamie and Edmund fault Tyrone, but unfairly in Mary's opinion. Each member of the family is accused on at least one occasion and exonerated on another.

TYRONE: I'm not blaming her.

JAMIE: (*Bitingly.*) Then who are you blaming? Edmund, for being born?

TYRONE: You damned fool! No one was to blame.

JAMIE: The bastard of a doctor was! From what Mama's said, he was another cheap quack like Hardy! You wouldn't pay for a first-rate—

TYRONE: That's a lie! (*Furiously.*) So I'm to blame! That's what you're driving at, is it? (29)

The litany of charges and counter-charges seems endless. Mary tells Edmund that of course he is not to blame (44) and neither is Jamie (64). "I blame only myself," she insists (87), but later she claims that none of us can help what happens.

Of the four Tyrones, James comes closest to the Aristotelian model of the tragic hero. "Fated" by childhood experience to flee from poverty, he overshot the mark. Given the circumstances of his life, his actions were predictable, but still, he is the one who chose. The family bears the indirect consequences of his decisions, and that he admits. Throughout the night Tyrone bears his sons' accusations with grudging acknowledgment, so that he eventually gains our understanding and even a measure of respect. Like Shakespeare's King Lear, Tyrone has dismembered his family, yet his suffering redeems him, and in the end he is reconciled with his most caring child. In another sense, however, that analogy is false. Lear is at the epicenter of disaster in Shakespeare's play, whereas the fault lines in *Long Day's Journey into Night* run everywhere. O'Neill does not determine the precise ratio of guilt and innocence in the Tyrone family. Instead, the play emphasizes the family's struggle to develop the dignity and resources they need to match their suffering in a world that forces bad decisions.

Eventually, the play throws its accusatory beam in all directions:

> It may have been all his fault in the beginning, but . . . (45)
> I'm not blaming you, dear (48)
> You're to blame, James (67)
> It's not you who should blame me (83)
> It was my fault (88)
> I don't blame you (93)
> I don't blame you a bit (108)
> So I'm to blame (111)
> Stop trying to blame him (119)
> Your stinginess is to blame (140)
> "The fault, dear Brutus" (152)
> I know that's not your fault, but . . . (166)

At the end of the play the question of who is at fault has lost most of its meaning. As John Henry Raleigh shrewdly puts it, in *Long Day's Journey into Night* "nothing is to blame except everybody."[63]

THE RIGHT KIND OF PITY

O'Neill's reluctance to point an accusing finger in the play almost certainly stems from his reliance on autobiographical materials. Because he drew upon his own family members as sources for his characters, he was compelled to struggle anew with the philosophical implications of human failure. He had already begun this process in *The Iceman Cometh*, where he developed a new conception of pity.

Central to *The Iceman Cometh* is a dispute between Hickey, the misguided protagonist, and his philosophical opponent, Larry Slade.

Believing that the forlorn drunkards who live and sleep in Harry Hope's bar are too weak to battle life, Larry chooses to accept them on their own terms and urges Hickey not to destroy their illusions. But Hickey contends that Larry's pity is the wrong kind because it demands too little of people. Hickey wants to disillusion the drunkards and force them to confront reality. He advocates "the right kind of pity," which is "after final results."[64] Yet in the course of the play Hickey is discredited. We learn that his wife's peculiar pity for him had driven him to the brink of insanity and that he murdered her out of hatred. For years he had been unfaithful to her, and for years she had coddled him, building up his illusion that one day he would reform and become a decent husband. Judging by the result, Evelyn's pity for Hickey was the wrong kind. O'Neill suggests that Evelyn's pity was manipulative, based on her position of moral superiority in their relationship; by feeding his illusions she controlled him. So, too, is Hickey's position flawed because he has been using Evelyn's tactic (in reverse) to motivate the roomers in the bar. His campaign to control their destiny fails. Thus Larry's position in the play is vindicated by default. O'Neill suggests that in certain cases, at least, it is better to respond to human weakness with simple compassion, regardless of blame and without pretense to superior knowledge.

The "right kind of pity" also is the issue at stake in *Long Day's Journey into Night*. Quoting one of Nietzsche's doleful proclamations, Edmund puts the concept on a metaphysical plane: " 'God is dead: of His pity for man hath God died' " (78). In its original context in *Thus Spoke Zarathustra* the passage continues: "But remember this also: all great love is lifted above all its pity; for it seeketh to create what it loveth!"[65] O'Neill copied out the entire passage in longhand in his notes, and it seems that the latter statement had special resonance for him. Like Nietzsche, O'Neill came to believe that the right kind of pity is demanding and creative. Commensurate with the greatest love, it elevates rather than lowers the person who is pitied in the estimation of the beholder. By contrast, the wrong kind of pity begins and ends in scorn. That kind of pity is commonplace; the other is godlike and exceedingly rare.

The Play as Tragedy

In *Long Day's Journey into Night* Mary remembers the right kind of pity from her convent days when the Blessed Virgin offered her "faith in Her love and pity" (94). Now that Mary's faith has weakened, she craves the same sustaining response from her family, but they are hard pressed to provide it. Jamie protests that he has "all the pity in the world for her" (76), but like Hickey's, his is the wrong kind, tainted by secret anger. Edmund and Tyrone come closer to the mark, but in the end they too fall short. Finally it is the playwright himself, hovering godlike above the stage, who strives to bring each member of the family into being "with deep pity and understanding and forgiveness" (dedication). His ultimate appeal is not to the characters on stage but to us.

Here, then, is O'Neill's most comprehensive reply to Aristotle. The aim of modern tragedy, like its classical counterpart, is to arouse pity and fear in the audience in order to enlarge our sympathies. But a playwright ought to school us in the higher pity that leads to understanding. Other forms of drama may school us in the easier variants of audience identification, such as outrage, scorn, and tearful sentiment, but tragedy offers a more stringent course. The right kind of pity demands a creative widening of our capacity to extend ourselves, to experience the suffering of those who are partly guilty as well as partly innocent so that we may come to terms with our own complicity in life.

THEATER OF FORGIVENESS

Not all critics agree that O'Neill fully succeeds in tempering his accusatory judgments in the play. Some suspect that his disappointment in his own mother leads him to shade his portrait of Mary with tones of disguised hostility.[66] And yet, O'Neill takes pains to create a reservoir of sympathy for Mary, as in the affecting scene between Mary and Cathleen at the beginning of the third act. In a long monologue Mary describes her earliest enthusiasms—for her father, for Mother Elizabeth, for the piano, for the holy life, and most of all, for her dashing young suitor. As we share this attractive moment from Mary's past, enjoying her experience as a shy, young girl in love, O'Neill builds our identification with Mary, preparing us to respond to her more charitably in the present.

O'Neill considerably softened the portrait of each family member as he revised.[67] For example, Tyrone's remark that it was years before he discovered what was wrong with Mary, implying that it was then too late to really help her, was an addition to the original manuscript, as was the stage direction that describes his tender cradling of her wedding dress. In the First Typescript O'Neill significantly extended Tyrone's fourth-act monologue, adding touches that mitigate our earlier impression of him as a heartless miser. Added brushstrokes also soften Jamie's character, an instance being his remembered distress at discovering Mary with a hypodermic needle.

Correspondingly, O'Neill deleted many cruel and rancorous speeches from the text. To cite but one example, Jamie admits in the manuscript draft that he entered his brother's room and infected him with measles out of jealousy, a confession that does not appear in the play. Indeed, it is touching to witness how the four Tyrones seem to become more acceptable to their creator as they progress through their incarnations in the drafts. It is as if O'Neill regarded his characters as souls in purgatory sloughing their worst sins until at last they were ready for the stage, where in their nakedness they could be forgiven. Mary is shriller and more vindictive in the drafts, Jamie more culpable, Tyrone more bitterly condemned. A number of the hostile exchanges that remain in the text are longer and even more vitriolic in the drafts. In the completed play the characters forgive more readily, and so do we. They lose track of who is to blame, and so do we. What is most extraordinary is the symmetry between O'Neill's process of composition and the refinement of our initial perception of his characters. Our responses seem orchestrated to recapitulate his revisions.

This same process occurs in each of the great plays that O'Neill completed after 1935. During this same period he abandoned *A Tale of Possessors Self-Dispossessed,* the cycle of eleven plays on the theme of national greed that caused him so much difficulty. Scholars have sought to explain the project's failure, citing the playwright's declining health and the enormous scope of the undertaking. A more subtle, spiritual process may have been at work, as well. A chronicle of moral wreckage and collective guilt, the cycle no longer harmonized with O'Neill's vision of forgiveness. At some level of awareness, O'Neill could not stir himself to revive the stony attitudes of his youth.

O'Neill helped to redefine modern tragedy, moving it away from the judgmental model toward something altogether new, the elegiac form adopted by his successors from Arthur Miller ("Nobody dast blame this man" [*Death of a Salesman*]) through Tennessee Williams, Edward Albee, Sam Shepard, Lanford Wilson, David Mamet, Marsha Norman, and August Wilson. But distinguishing the right from the wrong kind of pity is difficult, and American dramatists still are sorting out O'Neill's dramatic legacy.

Today the pendulum has swung far away from moral condemnation of the protagonist. The English-speaking stage is occupied by characters who are victims of a pathological social order or of biology gone awry. The maimed are everywhere: Bernard Pomerance's *The Elephant Man,* Mark Medoff's *Children of a Lesser God,* Brian Clark's *Whose Life Is It, Anyway?,* Arthur Kopit's *Wings.* Hospitals, old-age homes, and lunatic asylums are favorite theatrical settings now. If contemporary audiences no longer feel inclined to accept the premise of self-victimization, they have no trouble accepting the notion of unmerited suffering. Violence and illness have become potent metaphors for reactive characters and for playgoers alike. From this perspective, O'Neill may have been the last modern playwright to comprehend the balance between guilt and innocence, blame and incapacity, that tragedy requires. *Long Day's Journey into Night* demonstrates that moral judgment and forgiveness, far from being incompatible components, are the dynamic elements of the rarest and most demanding form of dramatic art.

THE PLAY AS AUTOBIOGRAPHY

9

A work of art is always happy; all else is unhappy.
        —O'Neill, letter to Malcolm Mollan, 1921

If we knew nothing about O'Neill's personal life, *Long Day's Journey into Night* would engage us on aesthetic grounds alone. Yet the connections between the playwright's art and experience are too compelling to ignore. According to his widow, O'Neill felt obliged to write this play if only to prevent some other dramatist from exploiting the raw material of his family background.[68] Of course, O'Neill rearranged chronology, withheld information, and in general shaped his reminiscence into a form that would justify a free-standing work of art. To treat the play merely as a collection of personal anecdotes would distort its artistic integrity.

In some respects *Long Day's Journey* has little in common with the formal conventions of narrative autobiography, which tends to focus on the author, with other characters entering the picture only as satellite figures. Teleology, or development toward a preconceived end, is usually the guiding principle in the author's disposition of events. However, in *Long Day's Journey* O'Neill truncates the arc of life. We

The Play as Autobiography

Left to right: Eugene, Jamie, and James O'Neill on the porch of Monte Cristo Cottage in New London, c. 1900. Photograph courtesy of the Collection of American Literature, Beinecke Rare Book and Manuscript Library, Yale University.

do not know whether Edmund lives on after 1912 or what becomes of the other family members. The play fixes a moment of time shared equally by its four protagonists, reaches into the past to illuminate that moment, and presents it without editorial comment. Thus we are free to generalize as we please. We may extend the lifelines of these characters if we wish to speculate about their futures, or we may break the dramatic illusion and apply to our own families whatever insights we have acquired. We do not need to know whether the play presents "facts" about "real people" in order to respond to a performance.

Still, anyone who has seen or read the play must be curious as to the parallels between the Tyrones and the O'Neills. How is the play connected to its roots? The relationship can be judged from a remarkable document that the playwright prepared in 1926. In nine dense paragraphs compressed onto a single sheet of paper in miniscule handwriting, O'Neill summarized his background for Dr. Gilbert V. Hamilton, a psychoanalyst whom he consulted briefly during this period.

Although never intended for public scrutiny, this document contains the germ of the plot for *Long Day's Journey into Night*.[69]

In the document O'Neill discusses his parents' marriage and the traumatic death of the couple's second child, describing the circumstances much as they are given in the play. Yet in the autobiographical summary O'Neill stresses the carelessness of his grandmother "in allowing older brother who has measles to see baby." He adds: "elder boy as direct cause, unconsciously(?)"—indicating by the question mark the ambiguity of Jamie's intention and the uncertain degree of his responsibility for the baby's death. Afterwards, the elder brother was sent away to school "at husband's command, despite M[other]'s protests as to his youth (seven)." The play makes no mention of such a quarrel.

After the banishment of her son, his mother was "absolutely alone," O'Neill writes, except for her husband, her poor relations in town, and a shiftless brother whom she despised. About this brother we hear nothing in the play, nor do we learn of a "series of brought-on abortions" that his mother underwent in defiance of her husband and her faith. The sixth paragraph of the autobiographical summary is the most poignant. It consists of two lines: "E. born with difficulty—M. sick but nurses child—starts treatment with Doc, which eventually winds up in start of nervousness, drinking & drug addiction. No signs of these before." The summary goes on to describe how the mother smothered her youngest son with affection, concentrating all her love on him in her loneliness, and how she pleaded with her husband for a home in New York, to no avail. The document ends by referring to a nurse in the household who became the mother's drinking companion and probably a messenger for obtaining drugs.

O'Neill, it seems, had no need to fabricate family incidents for his plot. He actually pruned additional family troubles from the finished play. In order to heighten dramatic unity and tension, he compressed chronology, moving his diagnosis of tuberculosis from the late fall of 1912 to August so it would coincide with one of his mother's drug episodes and so that the family would be together at the cottage. Actually, Jamie was absent from New London when O'Neill became ill, and his father was in New York filming a silent movie version of *The Count of Monte Cristo*. That year was indeed significant for the family. James O'Neill was ready to retire from the stage, and Eugene had just begun his career as a writer, working as a cub reporter on the New London *Telegraph* and also trying his hand at poetry. During that same year a nurse had to be summoned to guard Mrs. O'Neill, who suffered fits of weeping brought on by drugs and the memory of her second baby's death.[70] O'Neill recalled these events with anguish.

MONTE CRISTO COTTAGE

The O'Neill family cottage still stands at 325 Pequot Avenue in New London. Now registered as a National Landmark, it has been carefully restored—though the hedge blocking the house from the road seems to have grown a little taller since the days when Jamie O'Neill worked on it. As the visitor walks up the sloping lawn toward the entrance, the Thames River comes into view across the street. The cottage itself is a disorganized affair, a quirky two-story structure. Its most distinctive feature is an open porch with latticework that wraps around the house like a pretty package meant to disguise its meager contents. One summer's day at the turn of the century James O'Neill posed on this porch with his two sons for a photograph. The actor, relaxing, leans back in his rocking chair. Jamie, probably in his early twenties, sports a straw hat at a jaunty angle. Already he has the air of a cynic, while Eugene, at perhaps age twelve, buries his head in a book. It is not difficult to locate the precise spot where this photograph was taken. Visitors to Monte Cristo Cottage may have the ghostly sensation of walking onto the set of the play. (Photo reproduced p. 93.)

Inside the cottage the Victorian atmosphere is somewhat gloomy, despite the warm tones of walnut paneling and parquet floors. The front door opens directly to a hallway and stairs leading to the second floor. Upstairs the planks creak like the decks of an old schooner, as they probably did years ago when the boys listened for sounds of their mother wandering in and out of the small bedrooms and pacing the corridor. Downstairs, the living room, where the play takes place, is off to the side of the house. The room is small and completely paneled in dark, varnished pine: intimate, but a bad place to begin a quarrel. With its windows blocked by fog, this little sitting room might offer pleasure to a solitary reader, but it would seem a clammy cell to four acrimonious adults feuding during a long day and night.

A glance confirms that this is the same space that O'Neill described from memory and without hesitation in his opening stage directions. (The set description in the original manuscript shows few corrections, indicating his sharp recollection.) O'Neill did alter the dimensions of the room as he thought out his theatrical needs. On stage the space is expanded laterally to provide maneuverability for the actors. A screen door leading to the porch is placed where O'Neill describes it, and the rows of windows and spaces for furniture conform to their locations in the text. In the set, the wall that faces the side yard disappears to become the front of the stage, permitting the audience to look through the living room toward the middle part of the house.

Here O'Neill makes an interesting change. His stage directions call for *"two double doorways with portieres"* on the rear wall of the set (11). The double doorway on the right, we are told, leads to the front parlor where Mary's piano is located; the one on the left opens to a dark parlor in the rear of the house. In the cottage the double doorway on the right exists exactly as described. Through it visitors can see the front parlor (with a piano) and the handsome balustrade of the stairway leading to the second story. However, the single doorway to the left leading to the rear parlor is cramped and awkward. Originally it served as the exterior door of a little schoolhouse on the adjacent property. James joined this odd structure to the cottage as a cheap way to expand his living space. In picturing the set, O'Neill ignored this detail to facilitate the cast's entrances and exits. There happens to be another matching double doorway in the house that leads from the front parlor to the rear but is invisible from the living room. It seems that in his imagination O'Neill transposed these doors from one room to the other to suit his stage purpose.

Another discrepancy awaits the visitor. The Tyrones, we are told, use the doorway on the left as they pass through the rear parlor to the dining room for meals. But the O'Neills regularly ate at a boarding house a few blocks away. Such was their established habit by 1913. It is possible that during the summer of 1912 the O'Neills had their meals prepared at home; although the kitchen no longer exists, there used to be one attached to the back of the house. However, it is more likely that O'Neill invented Bridget the cook as a stage device. Certainly it would have been awkward to send the characters out of the house several times during the play for meals. O'Neill decided that the Tyrones must eat in, and perhaps that is why he provided them with an enlarged doorway to a dining room that was never used. Here as in many other instances the playwright in O'Neill overruled the autobiographer.[71]

MARY ELLEN ["ELLA"] QUINLAN O'NEILL (MARY): 1857–1922

James and Ella arrived in New London in 1883 and soon purchased the cottage and its surrounding property. They were drawn to New London because Ella's mother and several of her relatives resided there. (O'Neill's mother was known throughout her adult life as Ella, although Mary Ellen was her given name.) James also found the town an attractive choice, for it was closer to Broadway and less expensive than its fashionable rival, Newport, where wealthier New York residents spent the summer. The town had a pleasant harbor, well-kept homes, and a number of tourist amenities. But as O'Neill's biographers report, Ella Quinlan O'Neill never felt comfortable in New London. After her mother died in 1887, Ella felt increasingly isolated, although she had a cousin living nearby. By then James had become a local celebrity. He spent a good many evenings being entertained by friends, while Ella, who refused to mix, felt excluded. Even before O'Neill's birth and its disastrous consequences, she already had withdrawn from town life.

Ella O'Neill did keep her wedding dress in a trunk in the attic, and from time to time she would bring it downstairs.[72] Moreover, at St.

Mary's Academy in Indiana, which Ella attended from 1872–75, she won a gold medal in music and was praised for her piano playing by a teacher named Mother Elizabeth. However, Mary's recollection of visiting "the shrine of Our Lady of Lourdes on the little island in the lake" (175) came not from Ella's life but from O'Neill's memory of such a spot at the Catholic boarding school in New York where he was sent as a boy.[73]

The chronology of Mary's first meeting with James Tyrone re-arranges the facts as they apply to O'Neill's parents. Mary reports that she first saw James Tyrone backstage after a performance to which her father had taken her in 1876. However, James O'Neill first met Ella at her father's home in 1872. Two years later Thomas Quinlan suddenly died from tuberculosis aggravated by alcoholism. When Ella met James again—true enough, backstage after a New York performance in 1876—it was at her own initiative. Her father, two years dead, had no hand in helping plan their marriage, as Mary's father is said to have done in the play. Either O'Neill was mistaken about the dates or he altered the chronology to emphasize Mary's innocence as a young woman. In the play Mary passes helplessly from her father's hands into her husband's; she is depicted as more timorous than Ella Quinlan was when she and James O'Neill became engaged.[74]

Ella and James were married on 14 June 1877. Their first child, James, Jr., was born the following year in San Francisco, where James was on tour. In 1883 Edmund, their second son, was born in St. Louis. Road life was a feature of James's profession, and Ella felt obliged to accompany her husband whenever possible. Often she left the children in the care of her mother in a New York apartment, and that is where Edmund contracted measles from Jamie during the winter of 1885. Ella was in Denver, where James was playing in *The Count of Monte Cristo*. By the time she was able to get back to New York, her infant son was dead. O'Neill's second wife, Agnes Boulton, recalled Ella speaking of this incident many years later, still blaming herself: "He might not have died if I hadn't left him."[75]

Eugene's birth in 1888 was, as the play recounts, the indirect cause of Ella's addiction. Whether the doctor who introduced her to morphine was a cheap hotel quack, as Mary charges in the play, or a respectable practitioner, cannot be ascertained. Drug addiction was a poorly understood phenomenon in the 1880s. At the time, some derivatives of morphine were available without prescription as over-the-counter drugs. Easy access explains why Ella had little difficulty replenishing her supply. The harmful effects of cocaine similarly were misjudged; in the 1880s Freud experimented with the narcotic as a cure-all. The drug could be found as an ingredient in a number of patent medicines and even (some suspect) in the early formula for Coca-Cola. Not until the Harrison Act of 1914 were narcotics in this country brought under strict control.

It is likely that O'Neill discovered his mother's condition in the summer of 1903, when he was almost fifteen. According to Louis Sheaffer, O'Neill's biographer, Ella tried to drown herself in the river that summer because she had run out of drugs.[76] O'Neill strongly identified with his mother; like her, he was abnormally nervous. His discovery must have been not only disillusioning but personally worrisome: O'Neill probably wondered whether the future held in store for him a similar dismal prospect. As luck would have it, he did inherit from his mother the tremor that eventually crippled him. Years later he bemoaned the Quinlan "heritage of God knows how long a line of people with high-strung nerves" (*Selected Letters*, 465).

There is a remarkable ending to Ella's life story. She not only recovered her faith but conquered her drug habit. Multiple sojourns in sanatoriums had failed, but in the spring of 1914 Ella retired to a convent where, with the aid of the nuns, she found the strength to achieve a permanent cure. Her triumph was liberating. She weathered the death of her husband in 1920, and in the remaining two years of her life blossomed into a self-possessed, competent woman who busied herself sorting out his affairs.[77] One of her first decisions was to sell Monte Cristo Cottage, which she had always detested. Jamie immediately attached himself to his widowed mother and accompanied her wherever she traveled. He even stopped his drinking, citing her example as his inspiration. Jamie was with his mother when she died in California on 28 February 1922. He never had another sober day.

JAMES O'NEILL, JR. (JAMIE): 1878–1923

At the time of Ella's death, Jamie had been on the wagon for nearly two years. He quickly made up for lost time, ending his days in an alcoholics' ward. "Booze got him in the end," O'Neill reported. "It was a shame. He and I were terribly close to each other, but after my mother's death in 1922 he gave up all hold on life and simply wanted to die as soon as possible" (*Selected Letters*, 378). Jamie's binge began on the train ride from Los Angeles to New York accompanying his mother's body, which had to be shipped back east for burial. According to the account he gave his brother, he spent every night locked in his compartment with a prostitute. The story haunted O'Neill for years until he finally used it as the basis of *A Moon for the Misbegotten,* his last play.

The central event in *A Moon for the Misbegotten* is Jim Tyrone's confession to Josie Hogan of that nightmarish train ride. Jim could not forgive his mother for deserting him, he explains, and so he sought out a prostitute to punish her: "It was as if I wanted revenge because I'd been left alone—because I knew I was lost."[78] Jim's behavior in *A Moon for the Misbegotten* is entirely consistent with Jamie's in *Long Day's Journey into Night.* Again we see the seven-year-old with measles who defied a warning because he was angry with his mother for deserting him to join his father on a trip. Again we see the man who buried himself in Fat Violet's bosom on that evening in 1912 when his mother returned to drugs. But this final act is a sacrilege that deeply stains him, and he turns to Josie for shriving.

The portrait of Jamie in these two plays corresponds closely to O'Neill's brother. The measles episode, school expulsions, bitterness, drinking, whoring, and the train ride are the legacy of James O'Neill, Jr. For a psychologist inclined to pursue the theory that Jamie suffered from an unresolved Oedipus complex, the hints are buried not far below the surface. The most telling anecdote is Agnes Boulton's recollection of the real-life Jamie at age forty confiding to his brother how every morning he would sneak into the bathroom to smell his mother's perfumed bathwater: " 'The old bastard doesn't appreciate her even now. Sometimes I go into the bathroom and dip my hands into the water before it's all run out—ummm!' "[79] The incident matches in grotesqueness the behavior of the character in both plays.

Jim's confession in *A Moon for the Misbegotten* is designed to absolve him from past as well as recent sins. In *Long Day's Journey into Night* Mary never forgives Jamie for causing the death of his brother, but through Josie's intercession maternal forgiveness is secured. "*She* hears," Josie assures him. "I feel her in the moonlight, her soul wrapped in it like a silver mantle." And, Josie declares, "*She* forgives, do you hear me!... *She* loves and understands and forgives!" (99). With this benediction O'Neill was able to say good-bye to his tortured brother. Perhaps the playwright felt obliged to apologize to Jamie for his own survival. In life O'Neill did take the advice that Jamie gives Edmund in *Long Day's Journey into Night;* he cut himself loose from his brother to avoid being dragged down into the vortex. O'Neill launched a successful career, married, and even stopped drinking. In the last years of Jamie's life the relationship between the brothers had cooled. Jamie destroyed himself. Eugene thrived.

There is a puzzle that bears mention in this connection. Why did Eugene O'Neill trade names in *Long Day's Journey into Night* with Edmund, the brother he never knew? Perhaps this self-effacing gesture was the manifestation of a death wish; or perhaps O'Neill meant to symbolize his identification with his two brothers, the one who died as a child and James O'Neill, Jr., whose death-in-life is poignantly dramatized in the play.

JAMES O'NEILL (TYRONE): 1846–1920

Whereas Jamie in *Long Day's Journey into Night* seems closely drawn from life, there is some dispute as to the fairness of O'Neill's portrait of his father. Friends who remembered James O'Neill protested that his presentation as a miser in the play was inaccurate. They recalled the actor as an open and generous man who always was happy to provide a handout. In truth, James O'Neill subsidized his son's early writing, bought him a studio on the Provincetown dunes as a wedding gift, and left him a sizable legacy in his will. These do not appear to be the gestures of a tightfisted father. On the other hand, James's selection in 1912 of a state-run sanatorium for his tubercular son casts him in an unflattering light. In the play Tyrone behaves inconsistently in matters pertaining to money. In life James O'Neill exhibited similar contradictory tendencies.

In the play Tyrone relents after Edmund accuses him of planning to send him to a cheap institution. "You can choose any place you like!" Tyrone concedes. "Any place you like—within reason" (148). In reality Eugene first was sent to the state farm, but he rebelled after two days there. On 9 December 1912 O'Neill was admitted as a patient to the Fairfield County State Tuberculosis Sanatorium in Shelton, Connecticut. On 11 December he had himself discharged. O'Neill spent the next few weeks living with his parents in New York. Then, in a blinding snowstorm on Christmas Eve, he entered the Gaylord Farm Sanatorium in Wallingsford, Connecticut, accompanied by his father—a theatrical entrance if ever there was one. Gaylord, a nonprofit institution supported by private philanthropists, is described in the play: "There's such a pile of money behind it, they don't have to charge much" (149). O'Neill remained a patient at Gaylord until he was pronounced fit for release in June 1913. The cost at Shelton for those who were not indigent was four dollars a week; at Gaylord it was seven.[80]

One of the most serious charges in the play is Edmund's claim that his father has failed to pursue an aggressive cure for Mary, just as now he is stinting on medical care for him. Tyrone maintains in his defense that like everyone else, he knew little about drug addiction in the early days: "What did I know of morphine? It was years before I discovered what was wrong" (141). There is no reason to doubt his rejoinder, but Ella's affliction must have become obvious to James while Eugene was still a little boy. In an old bookstore a few years ago I came across a copy of The Dramatic Magazine, a trade journal for the theater published in Chicago, dated January 1900. The issue contains two interesting items, a full-page photograph of James O'Neill in his costume as D'Artagnan from The Musketeers and an ad for opium and morphine cures placed in the back pages by a Dr. Stephens of Lebanon, Ohio. Two conclusions may be drawn from this conjunction: certainly by 1900 readers and advertisers perceived drug addiction as a problem in the theatrical profession; and James O'Neill, who must have owned a copy of this magazine, could not have helped noticing the ad. The magazine is dated twelve years after Eugene's birth and twelve years before the events of *Long Day's Journey into Night*. Still, precisely dating James's recognition of his wife's illness (surely it was well before 1900) is impossible. The evidence suggests that while James clearly knew the nature of Ella's problem, he was helpless to alleviate it.

One incident in James's early life is glossed over quickly in the play. Mary makes a brief remark to Cathleen about a scandal that broke out shortly after her marriage, something to do with a lawsuit brought against James by a woman who had been his mistress (86). In life the woman who embarrassed the O'Neills was Nettie Walsh, a former girlfriend who brought a paternity suit against James two months after he married Ella. Eventually the lawsuit was dismissed, but not before a spate of ugly newspaper stories in the fall of 1877 dampened the newlyweds' honeymoon. Walsh claimed (falsely) that James had married and then abandoned her. One of O'Neill's biographers claims that James did sire Nettie's illegitimate son, but the evidence is less than conclusive.[81] Though entangled in love affairs as an unmarried actor, James became a model husband. Mary proudly asserts in the play that for thirty-six years Tyrone's fidelity has never wavered (105). O'Neill confirms this view in one of his letters, extolling his parents' deep, mutual love (*Selected Letters*, 132).

As recounted in the play, the highlight of James O'Neill's acting career occurred in Chicago when he played opposite the great Edwin Booth in *Othello*. Thanks to a playbill from McVicker's Theatre that James preserved in his personal scrapbook, we know the play opened with Booth playing Othello on 24 February 1874. "Jas. O'Neill" receives fourth billing as Iago after Booth and the two actresses who played Desdemona and Emelia. Then, in small print at the bottom of the program, the following notice appears: "Mr. BOOTH will appear as IAGO, on Friday, March 6th."[82] That must have been the first evening that James played the leading role in Booth's stead; in *Long Day's Journey into Night* Tyrone recounts that Booth exclaimed: "That young man is playing Othello better than I ever did!" (150).

The fatal turning point in the actor's career came in 1883, when James was offered the role of Edmond Dantes in *The Count of Monte Cristo*. "Imagine!" Eugene O'Neill told his friend Saxe Commins: "He played that part more than six thousand times, no wonder it made an addict out of [my mother]."[83] The figure of six thousand performances may be exaggerated, but James quickly became identified with the part and, despite sincere efforts to vary his repertoire, did little else for the next twenty-five years. Shortly before he died he confided to his son his bitter regret that he had wasted his talent. "How keenly he felt this in the last years," O'Neill explained, soon after his father passed away.

> His last words to me—when speech had almost failed him—were: 'Eugene—I'm going to a better sort of life. This sort of life—here— all froth—no good—rottenness!' This after seventy-six years of what the mob undoubtedly regard as a highly successful career! It furnishes food for thought, what? I have quoted his words verbatim. They are written indelibly—seared on my brain—a warning from Beyond to remain true to the best that is in me though the heavens fall. (*Selected Letters*, 143)

Years later when he wrote *Long Day's Journey into Night*, O'Neill transformed his father's deathbed message into that luminous moment in act 4 when Edmund responds to Tyrone's confession with his own pledge to remain true to the poet in him, no matter what the cost.

Eugene O'Neill (Edmund): 1888–1953

O'Neill's self-portrait in the play is somewhat disingenuous. Edmund Tyrone appears as a relatively inexperienced youth, but by 1912 Eugene O'Neill had fathered a child, divorced a wife, and logged a series of love affairs in addition to the hours he spent with Jamie at the local brothel. In the summer of 1912, while waiting for his divorce to be finalized, O'Neill was courting an attractive New London girl named Maibelle Scott, but there is no sign in the play of any particular romantic interest in Edmund's life. Why did O'Neill suppress these details yet draw freely from his family history in shaping his character studies for the other Tyrones? One obvious answer, of course, is that O'Neill was reluctant to expose the episode of his failed marriage. Yet there is an artistic purpose to consider also. Edmund's inexperience in the play is crucial: through his passivity the family's aggression comes sharply into focus. The dynamic of O'Neill's stage family would significantly change were Edmund presented as a man who had a former wife and child to worry about. In that circumstance his struggle to escape his mother's influence would appear in a different light.

The facts are these. O'Neill met Kathleen Jenkins in the spring of 1909. When she discovered that she was pregnant, he agreed to a pro forma marriage to legitimize their child. The marriage ceremony took place in secret on 2 October 1909. Two weeks later O'Neill set sail for Honduras ostensibly to prospect for gold but in reality to escape the marriage. The couple never set up house, and O'Neill did not meet the son that was born of this union (Eugene O'Neill, Jr.) until the boy was twelve. From 1909 to 1912 O'Neill's life was in turmoil. In *Long Day's Journey into Night* Jamie refers to "all the crazy stunts [Edmund] has pulled in the last few years—working his way all over the map as a sailor and all that stuff" (35). The reality was more sordid than romantic. O'Neill drank heavily, shunned his wife and child, and bummed around Latin America, hitting bottom in Buenos Aires in 1911. Returning to New York, he went through the motions of allowing himself to be caught with a prostitute in order to provide Kathleen with legal grounds for a divorce. That event transpired in late December 1911. O'Neill then was living (largely on a liquid diet) in a combination bar and rooming house known as Jimmy the Priest's, and in January he attempted suicide there by taking an overdose of a drug called veronal. (Edmund mentions this episode in act 4 of the play but provides no details.) In the aftermath of this fiasco, O'Neill reattached himself to his parents, joining his father and mother on James's annual road tour of *Monte Cristo*. Jamie was along as a member of the cast, and O'Neill reluctantly accepted bit parts in the play to earn his keep. At the end of the season, the family returned together to New London for the summer, and that is when the play takes place. O'Neill's self-destructive behavior during this period appears to have had several causes—anxiety over his mother's addiction, guilt stemming from his marital troubles, and his despair of ever becoming a recognized poet. The following Christmas he entered Gaylord, where he slowly regained his health and began to put his life in order.[84]

In 1918 O'Neill married again. This union, to Agnes Boulton, endured ten years, until he fell in love with the actress Carlotta Monterey. In his letter to Agnes asking for a divorce, O'Neill eerily employed the same self-serving phrase that he gives to Mary in *Long Day's Journey into Night*: "Neither of us is to blame. It is life which has made us what we are" (*Selected Letters*, 271). Perhaps O'Neill, when writing the letter, remembered a phrase that he had learned from his mother, or perhaps he drew upon his own weakness as a husband when he gave the line to Mary in the play.

O'Neill's personal life lends credence to Mary's view that we all are victims of our family inheritance. O'Neill harshly rejected not only Agnes, but his two children by her, Shane and Oona. At first O'Neill admitted that when he thought of the children he suffered "like hell from a sense of guilt toward them." But soon he was speaking of Shane as just another "parasitic slob of a Boulton," stating that "son or not, he simply does not interest me as a human being" (*Selected Letters*, 281, 483). In the play Mary expresses animosity toward her sons as a defensive/aggressive response to her own guilt feelings for letting them down. Again, was O'Neill reflecting on his own failed relationship with his children when he wrote portions of *Long Day's Journey into Night*? Or was he repeating in life the family pattern implicit in the play? His father's father abandoned his wife and children to return to Ireland. His father denied paternity to Nettie Walsh's son. O'Neill himself abandoned a wife and son before he married Agnes Boulton, and in the wake of their divorce he abandoned his children again.

Ironically, O'Neill once copied out in longhand this passage from *Thus Spoke Zarathustra:* "Unto my children shall I make amends for being the child of my fathers."[85] He failed pitifully to achieve that goal. His two sons killed themselves. Eugene O'Neill, Jr., who became a classics professor and an expert on tragedy, slit his wrists in his bath (Roman fashion) three years before his father died. Shane, who never understood his father's rejection, became an alcoholic like his Uncle Jamie and then a drug addict like his grandmother. He jumped to his death from an apartment window in New York in 1977. Only Oona escaped. Unable to keep her father's love, she fled from the greatest tragedian of the age to the greatest comedian, marrying Charlie Chaplin (who was her father's age) in 1943. As a result, O'Neill disinherited her. Although he could forgive the dead in *Long Day's Journey into Night,* he never could forgive the living.

Richard Armour, the humorist, once quipped: "After reading a biography of O'Neill, one not only understands his tragedies better but finds them a relief."[86] Actually, not all was doom and darkness for the O'Neills. There were moments of triumph in store for the family that could not have been predicted from the ending of the play: each of the four O'Neills lived to see a major wish fulfilled. James watched his son develop into the fine artist that he might have been, Ella conquered her addiction, and for a few years Jamie finally had his mother all to himself. As for O'Neill, his third marriage was a fulfilling one despite its stormy quarrels. With Carlotta Monterey he had no children; instead she devoted herself to creating the ideal conditions for his work, and they lived exclusively for art.

O'Neill dedicated *Long Day's Journey into Night* to Carlotta on their twelfth wedding anniversary. "I mean it as a tribute to your love and tenderness," he wrote, "which gave me the faith in love that enabled me to face my dead at last and write this play."

THE PLAYWRIGHT NODDED

══ 10 ══

Throughout their marriage Carlotta Monterey O'Neill served as her husband's secretary. Occasionally she made mistakes. In *Long Day's Journey into Night* several lines in the original typescript are missing in the play.[87] For example, as the text now reads, Edmund quarrels with his mother about Dr. Hardy at the end of the second act, then goes off without saying good-bye. But that is not the ending of the scene as O'Neill wrote it.

The text of *Long Day's Journey into Night* is based on a second typescript of the play that Carlotta produced in the early 1940s. She first typed a copy of her husband's pencil manuscript, which itself contained revisions. O'Neill then edited this draft, making extensive cuts. It was from this heavily edited first typescript that the second typescript was prepared. O'Neill presumably read the second type-script, which became the source of the printed text, but his proofreading was lax. He failed to notice several "clean" omissions—lines definitely not marked for deletion in the first typescript but which Carlotta accidentally dropped during her retyping. One of these was caught by Judith Barlow in her 1985 study of O'Neill's composition process.[88] Barlow noticed that Edmund does bid good-bye to his mother at the end of the second act; the line had been overlooked by Carlotta.

In my research for this study, I have discovered three additional missing lines that evidently suffered the same mishap. The most important of these is another lost line by Edmund that occurs on the same page as his missing good-bye. At the end of the second act the men are getting ready to leave for town: Tyrone for his club, Edmund and Jamie to visit Dr. Hardy, where they expect bad news regarding Edmund's "summer cold." Mary warns Edmund not to let Jamie take him drinking. Doesn't he know what Dr. Hardy has said concerning alcohol? Edmund replies bitterly: "I thought he was an old idiot" (94). In the text, Mary rebukes Edmund (or so it seems) for his remark about Hardy. "*Pitifully*" she calls out Edmund's name. But the printed text makes little sense. Throughout the play Mary expresses contempt for Hardy and is quick to agree with anyone who has a bad word to say about doctors; it was Mary herself who called Hardy an old idiot a few minutes earlier. Her reaction seems out of character.

However, Mary's rebuke makes perfect sense in response to the missing line that Edmund hurls at her in the first typescript: "I thought he was an old idiot. *Anyway, by tonight what will you care?*" (First Typescript, 2:2:16; my italics). The lost line significantly changes the emotional tenor of the scene. In context, Mary's pitiful cry is not meant for Edmund and certainly not for Dr. Hardy, but for herself.

"Anyway, by tonight what will you care?" marks a turning point in the play. Edmund, who has defended his mother until now, joins his father and brother in attacking Mary for her relapse into drug addiction. Indeed, this is the sharpest line that Edmund has spoken to her since the play began. Because he wounds her deeply, Edmund's conciliatory "Goodbye, Mama" (also missing from the printed text) is necessary to undo the hurt. As O'Neill builds to the climax of the scene, these missing elements are integral to Mary's emotional pitch. With Edmund now against her, as well as Jamie and her husband, Mary's famous curtain line a moment later is more poignant in its full context: "Then Mother of God, why do I feel so lonely?" (95).

Is it possible that lines as important as these really were lost from the play without O'Neill's notice? Indeed, how do we know that O'Neill did not cut them intentionally from the second typescript? The evidence is compelling that these lines *were* lost by mistake. My conclusions are based on the physical evidence (the first typescript very carefully indicates deletions and additions, whereas the second typescript is clean); on the dramatic context of the missing lines; and, finally, on a telling anecdote by Donald Gallup, the former curator of the O'Neill Collection at the Beinecke Rare Book and Manuscript Library at Yale University.

Gallup reports that Fredric March, who played James Tyrone in the 1956 American premiere of the play, approached him during rehearsal with a question that was puzzling the cast. No one knew how to interpret a line spoken by Jamie in the fourth act: "God bless you, K.O." Who was K.O.? The initials made no sense. Gallup consulted the original manuscript, which was in his care, and discovered that Carlotta had dropped an entire line during her typing. What Jamie says to his brother before he passes out is: "God bless you, Kid. *His eyes close. He mumbles.* That last drink—the old K.O." O'Neill never caught the error. Gallup delivered the line to the cast and made the correction in the fifth printing of the Yale University Press edition.[89]

It seems that Carlotta made similar errors in the second typescript. In the case of the second act, she had reached the bottom of a page when she began typing Edmund's speech with its first line, "I thought he was an old idiot." She stopped, put a new sheet in the typewriter and simply lost her place. Did she sense something amiss and then in her distraction lose Edmund's tender good-bye as well? Whatever the cause, she nodded. So did the playwright as he skimmed her copy, and the error was enshrined in the text. As a result, no one until now has ever heard the ending of act 2 as O'Neill wrote it. The first typescript contains a more powerful curtain than the one we've known.[90]

CURTAIN DOWN
11

As we leave the theater, we may say to ourselves that if we study the dysfunctional patterns of the Tyrones, perhaps we will learn how to negotiate our own problems. But the central question raised by *Long Day's Journey into Night* is unanswerable. Can we overcome our emotional failures through insight, or does the past largely control our responses? As Mary says, some things in life are "done before you realize it, and once they're done they make you do other things until . . ." (61). Publicly as Americans we deny that claim; we resist the idea of inexorability in life, preferring to believe that anyone can start over tomorrow if he or she really wants to. Privately, we have our doubts.

That is why we are transfixed by the freight of sorrow in O'Neill's biography and search the wreckage for clues to his accomplishment. Why did beauty emerge from his particular pain? The obvious explanation cannot be trusted—compensation for a mother's drug addiction, a brother's alcoholism, a father's failed career, loss of religious belief, physical infirmities, abandoned children, death wish, and the rest. The details of O'Neill's intimate life are fascinating, but we cannot say what helped him to become a playwright or by what alchemy he transformed sorrow into eloquence. When we shift our glance from autobiography to art, we are confronted with mystery.

Notes

1. Quoted by Edward T. Herbert, "Eugene O'Neill: An Evaluation by Fellow Playwrights," *Modern Drama* 6 (1963):239.

2. Louis Sheaffer, *O'Neill: Son and Playwright* (Boston: Little, Brown & Co., 1968), 477.

3. Jackson Bryer, ed., *"The Theater We Worked For": The Letters of Eugene O'Neill to Kenneth Macgowan* (New Haven: Yale University Press, 1982), 191.

4. Seymour Peck, "A Talk with Mrs. O'Neill," *O'Neill and His Plays: Four Decades of Criticism,* ed. Oscar Cargill, N. Bryllion Fagin, and William Fisher (New York: New York University Press, 1961), 93.

5. The following account is based on Eugene O'Neill's *Work Diary: 1924–1943*, vol. 2, Preliminary Edition, transcribed by Donald Gallup (New Haven: Yale University Library, 1981); hereafter cited in the text by date of entry. For further discussion of O'Neill's composition process see Virginia Floyd, ed., *Eugene O'Neill at Work: Newly Released Ideas for Plays* (New York: Frederick Ungar Publishing Co., 1981), 281–97, and Judith Barlow, *Final Acts: The Creation of Three Late O'Neill Plays* (Athens: University of Georgia Press, 1985), 63–111.

6. Virginia Floyd, ed., *The Unfinished Plays: Notes for The Visit of Malatesta, The Last Conquest, Blind Alley Guy* (New York: Frederick Ungar, 1988), 195.

7. *Work Diary,* 2:403.

8. Barlow, *Final Acts,* note, 178.

9. Carlotta O'Neill's remarks in conversation as reported by José Quintero, "Carlotta and the Master," *New York Times Magazine,* 1 May 1988, 66.

10. Dorothy Commins, ed., *"Love and Admiration and Respect": The O'Neill-Commins Correspondence* (Durham: Duke University Press, 1986), 201.

11. Dorothy Commins in a letter to the author, 31 August 1987.

12. For a discussion of the Swedish opening of the play see Tom Olsson, "O'Neill and the Royal Dramatic," *Eugene O'Neill: A World View,* ed. Virginia Floyd (New York: Frederick Ungar, 1979), 43–51.

13. Walter Kerr, "*Long Day's Journey into Night,*" reprinted in *Playwright's Progress: O'Neill and the Critics,* ed. Jordan Y. Miller (Chicago: Scott, Foresman & Co., 1965), 137.

14. John Chapman, "*Long Day's Journey into Night,*" reprinted in Miller, ed., *Playwright's Progress,* 134.

15. Quoted by Jordan Y. Miller, *Eugene O'Neill and the American Critic: A Bibliographical Checklist,* 2d ed. rev. (Hamden, Conn.: Archon Books, 1973), 368.

16. Henry Hewes, "*Long Day's Journey into Night,*" reprinted in *O'Neill and His Plays,* ed. Cargill, 218.

17. Quoted by Miller, *Eugene O'Neill and the American Critic,* 369.

18. Quoted in ibid., 370.

19. Mervyn Rothstein, "Quintero and O'Neill: Two Lives Entwined," *New York Times,* 16 June 1988, 19.

20. Frank Rich, "The Stars Align for *Long Day's Journey, New York Times,* 15 June 1988, 19.

21. Robert Brustein, *The Theatre of Revolt: An Approach to Modern Drama* (Boston: Little, Brown & Co., 1964), 359.

22. Eric Bentley, *Theatre of War: Modern Drama from Ibsen to Brecht* (New York: Viking Press, 1973), 71–75.

23. Eric Bentley, *The Playwright as Thinker* (1947; reprint, New York: Meridian Books, 1960), 272.

24. For a convenient introduction to diverse critical approaches to the play see Harold Bloom, ed., *Eugene O'Neill's "Long Day's Journey into Night"* (New York: Chelsea House, 1987).

25. For a recent feminist interpretation of the play see Bette Mandl, "Wrestling with the Angel in the House: Mary Tyrone's Long Journey," *The Eugene O'Neill Newsletter* 12, no. 3 (1988):19–23.

26. See Steven F. Bloom, "Empty Bottles, Empty Dreams: O'Neill's Use of Drinking and Alcoholism in *Long Day's Journey into Night,*" *Critical Essays on Eugene O'Neill,* ed. James Martine (Boston: G.K. Hall & Co., 1984), 159–77, and Gloria Dibble, "A Family Disease," *Eugene O'Neill Newsletter* 9 (1985):12–14.

27. John Henry Raleigh, "O'Neill's *Long Day's Journey into Night* and New England Irish-Catholicism," reprinted in *O'Neill: A Collection of Critical Essays,* ed. John Gassner (Englewood Cliffs, N.J.: Prentice-Hall, 1964), 124.

Notes

28. Leo Tolstoy, *Anna Karenina,* trans. Aylmer Maude, ed. George Gibian (New York: W. W. Norton, 1970), 1.

29. Quoted in *O'Neill and His Plays,* ed. Cargill et al., 111.

30. Egil Törnqvist suggests that the back parlor represents "the guilt and misery of the past; no one wants to dwell in it; yet all must occasionally pass through it" (Egil Törnqvist, *A Drama of Souls: Studies in O'Neill's Super-Naturalistic Technique* [New Haven: Yale University Press, 1969], 76).

31. A point observed in passing by Travis Bogard, *Contour in Time: The Plays of Eugene O'Neill* (New York: Oxford University Press, 1972), 424.

32. This memorandum appears on a loose page among O'Neill's manuscript notes for *Long Day's Journey into Night* in the Eugene O'Neill Collection, Collection of American Literature, Beinecke Rare Book and Manuscript Library, Yale University. Reproduced in a condensed version by Floyd, *Eugene O'Neill at Work,* 292.

33. Ernest Dowson, "*Vita summa brevis spem nos vetat incohare longum,*" *The Poems of Ernest Dowson,* ed. Mark Longaker (Philadelphia: University of Pennsylvania Press, 1962), 38.

34. An entry for 19 February 1940 reads: "Idea orchestral technique for a play—playwright as leader of symphony, characters, chorus, as orchestra (notes)" (O'Neill, *Work Diary,* 371).

35. Floyd, ed., *Eugene O'Neill at Work,* 228.

36. For a detailed chart of the plays' major motifs as keyed to each character see Michael Manheim, *Eugene O'Neill's New Language of Kinship* (Syracuse, N.Y.: Syracuse University Press, 1982), appendix, 211–17.

37. Nancy L. Roberts and Arthur W. Roberts, eds., *The Letters of Eugene O'Neill to George Jean Nathan* (Rutherford, N.J.: Fairleigh Dickinson University Press, 1987), 202.

38. Törnqvist, *A Drama of Souls,* 96–97.

39. According to James A. Robinson, Mary is a hypocrite and the chief sinner of the play (*Eugene O'Neill and Oriental Thought: A Divided Vision* [Carbondale: Southern Illinois University Press, 1982], 178).

40. Barlow suggests that Mary's ambivalence toward her mother contributes to her uneasiness with the maternal role (*Final Acts,* 88).

41. Floyd makes a similar point about Mary's escapism in *The Plays of Eugene O'Neill: A New Assessment* (New York: Frederick Ungar, 1985), 539. For a general discussion of Mary's romanticism see also Rolf Sheibler, *The Late Plays of Eugene O'Neill* (Bern: Francke Verlag, 1970), 107–17.

42. Bogard touches on this point in *Contour in Time,* 431. On the matter of Jamie's habits of quotation see Jean Chothia, *Forging a Language: A Study of the Plays of Eugene O'Neill* (Cambridge: Cambridge University Press, 1979), 177.

43. The point is noted by Sheibler in *The Late Plays of Eugene O'Neill*, 127.

44. For a discussion of the Oedipus complex consult Sigmund Freud, *A General Introduction to Psycho-Analysis*, trans. Joan Riviere (New York: Simon & Schuster, 1935), 281–96, and also Freud's "The Passing of the Oedipus-Complex," in *Sexuality and the Psychology of Love*, ed. Philip Rieff (New York: Collier Books, 1963), 176–82. For several provocative discussions of *Long Day's Journey into Night* in this context see the following: Bogard, *Contour in Time*, 435–44; Sheibler, *The Late Plays of Eugene O'Neill*, 125–28; Törnqvist, *A Drama of Souls*, 239–40. See also Philip Weisman, *Creativity in the Theater: A Psychoanalytic Study* (New York: Delta, 1965), 113–45. Whether O'Neill intended to suggest an Oedipal pattern in his portrait of Jamie remains an open question. O'Neill was familiar with Freud's writings and at one point briefly underwent psychoanalysis himself. Yet he remarked to a friend: "There is no conscious use of psychoanalytical material in any of my plays. . . . It was dramatic instinct and my own personal experience with human life that guided me" (quoted by Leonard Chabrowe, *Ritual and Pathos: The Theater of O'Neill* [Cranbury, N.J.: Associated University Presses, 1976], 103).

45. These parallels are suggested by Törnqvist, *A Drama of Souls*, 239–40.

46. Bogard, *Contour in Time*, 435.

47. Barlow, *Final Acts*, 107.

48. First typewritten draft of *Long Day's Journey into Night*, copy of revised manuscript, with the author's handwritten revisions, the Eugene O'Neill Collection, Collection of American Literature, Beinecke Rare Book and Manuscript Library, Yale University Library, p. 21. Hereafter cited parenthetically as First Typescript.

49. Robert Einenkel, "Long Day's Journey toward Separation: The Mary-Edmund Struggle," *The Eugene O'Neill Newsletter* 9 (1985):14.

50. Bogard presses the Jamie/Edmund parallel to suggest that in *Long Day's Journey into Night* O'Neill may have depicted his brother as a double of himself: by dramatizing Jamie's Oedipal dilemma, O'Neill may have been trying to come to terms with his own (*Contour in Time*, 436–40).

51. O'Neill in a letter to Barrett Clark. Travis Bogard and Jackson R. Bryer, ed., *Selected Letters of Eugene O'Neill* (New Haven: Yale University Press, 1988), 87. Subsequent references to this volume are cited in the text as *Selected Letters*.

52. O'Neill to Arthur Hobson Quinn, quoted in *O'Neill and His Plays*, ed. Cargill et al., 463.

53. "Second Thoughts," *The American Spectator*, December 1932, 2.

54. Chothia, *Forging a Language*, 207.

Notes

55. Algernon Charles Swinburne, "A Leave-Taking," in *Poems and Ballads,* ed. Morse Peckham (Indianapolis: Bobbs-Merrill Co., 1970), 56.

56. Unbound handwritten note by O'Neill filed with the manuscript material for *Long Day's Journey into Night,* Beinecke Rare Book and Manuscript Library, Yale University.

57. Tyrone's "Ingratitude, the vilest weed that grows" (32) is a distortion of Lear's "Ingratitude, thou marble-hearted fiend" (*King Lear,* 1:4:281). In act 4, his remark to Edmund that his son is "A poor thing but mine own" (143) is a mistaken rendering of "an ill-favored thing, sir, but mine own" from *As You Like It* (5:4:60). Jamie similarly commits an error when he alludes to "Old Gaspard, the miser in 'The Bells'" (158). In Leopold Lewis's 1871 melodrama *The Bells,* the greedy Alsatian Burgomaster who murders a Jew for his gold is named Mathias, not Gaspard.

58. Oscar Wilde, "The Ballad of Reading Gaol," *Poems by Oscar Wilde* (London: Methuen, 1909), 272.

59. Ibid., 298.

60. Ernest Dowson, "*Non Sum Qualis Eram Bonae Sub Regno Cynarae,*" *The Poems of Ernest Dowson,* ed. Longaker, 58.

61. For example, see Sheibler, *The Late Plays of Eugene O'Neill,* 126.

62. Aristotle, *Poetics,* trans. S. H. Butcher, with an introduction by Francis Fergusson (New York: Hill & Wang Dramabook, 1961), 76.

63. Raleigh, "O'Neill's *Long Day's Journey into Night* and New England Irish-Catholicism," 125.

64. *The Iceman Cometh* (New York: Random House, 1946), 2:116–17.

65. The passage is from a section of Nietzsche's *Thus Spoke Zarathustra* entitled "On the Pitying." For the complete passage, see *The Viking Portable Nietzsche,* ed. Walter Kaufmann (New York: Viking, 1954), 202. Among O'Neill's manuscript notes at the Beinecke Library at Yale are eight pages of handwritten quotations from *Thus Spoke Zarathustra,* including this quotation.

66. Floyd, for example, claims that Mary is portrayed as "selfish, vindictive, vengeful, and irresponsible." Nowhere in O'Neill's canon, she adds, "does he absolve his mother" (*The Plays of Eugene O'Neill: A New Assessment,* 542, 582).

67. This important insight is well documented by Barlow in *Final Acts,* 63–111.

68. "He said, 'I've got to write this. I'm afraid someone might find out about us one day and write something vulgar and melodramatic about it, even make a play out of it. But it was never vulgar!'" Quoted by Louis Sheaffer, "Eugene O'Neill: At Home in New London," *Milwaukee Repertory Theater Program,* 24 January 1977, 13. On matters about which O'Neill's biographers

117

disagree, I follow the authority of Louis Sheaffer throughout this chapter, unless otherwise noted.

69. This autobiographical sketch has been reproduced (with a few minor inaccuracies) by Louis Sheaffer in the second volume of his biography of the playwright, *O'Neill: Son and Artist* (Boston: Little, Brown & Co., 1973), 510–12. The manuscript is owned by a private collector, Dr. Harley Hammerman of Creve Coeur, Missouri. I am grateful to Dr. Hammerman for allowing me to examine a photocopy of the original document and to quote from it here.

70. Sheaffer, *O'Neill: Son and Playwright*, 19.

71. I am indebted to Sally Pavetti, curator of Monte Cristo Cottage, for her helpful comments on these matters.

72. Croswell Bowen, *Curse of the Misbegotten: A Tale of the House of O'Neill* (New York: Ballantine Books, 1959), 29.

73. Arthur Gelb and Barbara Gelb, *O'Neill* (New York: Delta, 1964), 69.

74. Gelb and Gelb, *O'Neill*, 15; Sheaffer, *O'Neill: Son and Playwright*, 13–15.

75. Agnes Boulton, *Part of a Long Story* (Garden City, N.Y.: Doubleday & Co., 1958), 233.

76. Louis Sheaffer, "Correcting Some Errors in Annals of O'Neill," *Comparative Drama* 17 (1983):209–10.

77. Sheaffer, *O'Neill: Son and Playwright*, 280–81; Gelb and Gelb, *O'Neill*, 433–34. Stephen Black wonders whether the passage of the Harrison Narcotics Act in 1914 forced Ella to take control of her life. No longer could she obtain drugs; she either had to cure herself or become an outlaw. Black also suggests that by 1914 Ella had completed menopause. Her morphine habit, he supposes, was largely an excuse to retreat from sexual relations so as to avoid another pregnancy; now she was free of that worry and so found means to effect a cure (Stephen A. Black, "Ella O'Neill's Addiction," *The Eugene O'Neill Newsletter* 14 [1985]:24–26).

78. *A Moon for the Misbegotten* (New York: Vintage Books, 1974), 98. Additional page references are cited in the text.

79. Boulton, *Part of a Long Story*, 210.

80. Gelb and Gelb, *O'Neill*, 220–25; Sheaffer, *O'Neill: Son and Playwright*, 242–47.

81. Doris Alexander, *The Tempering of Eugene O'Neill* (New York: Harcourt, Brace, & World, 1962), 7–10. Regarding the Nettie Walsh affair, see also Gelb and Gelb, *O'Neill*, 32–33; Sheaffer, *O'Neill: Son and Playwright*, 11–12, 74.

82. The playbill is part of James O'Neill's *Scrapbook* in the Eugene O'Neill Collection, Collection of American Literature, Beinecke Rare Book and Manuscript Library, Yale University Library.

Notes

83. *The O'Neill-Commins Correspondence*, ed. Commins, 24.

84. Boulton, *Part of a Long Story*, 196–206; Gelb and Gelb, *O'Neill*, 131–43, 173, 186–90; Sheaffer, *O'Neill: Son and Playwright*, 144–221; Sheaffer, "O'Neill's First Wife Defamed," *The Eugene O'Neill Newsletter* 9 (1985):27.

85. "Nietzsche Quotations," the Eugene O'Neill Collection, Collection of American Literature, Beinecke Rare Book and Manuscript Library, Yale University Library.

86. Richard Armour, *American Lit Relit* (New York: McGraw-Hill Book Co., 1964), 145.

87. I discuss these matters in greater detail in "Missing Lines in *Long Day's Journey into Night*," *Modern Drama* 22 (1989):179–82. I am grateful to the editors of *Modern Drama* for permission to include a portion of that material here.

88. Barlow, *Final Acts*, 73.

89. Donald Gallup, "The Eugene O'Neill Collection at Yale," *The Eugene O'Neill Newsletter* 9 (1985):5–6.

90. In 1989, Yale University Press issued a corrected edition of the play, which restores the missing lines.

Selected Bibliography

Primary Works

"As Ever, Gene": The Letters of Eugene O'Neill to George Jean Nathan. Edited by Arthur W. and Nancy L. Roberts. Cranbury, N.J.: Associated University Presses, 1987. Letters from O'Neill to the prominent drama critic, who was a friend.

Eugene O'Neill at Work: Newly Released Ideas for Plays. Edited by Virginia Floyd. New York: Frederick Ungar, 1981. Invaluable compendium of O'Neill's notes, ideas, outlines. Annotated.

Eugene O'Neill: Complete Plays. Edited by Travis Bogard. 3 vols. New York: Library of America, 1988. The first complete, standard edition of the plays.

Eugene O'Neill: Poems 1912–1944. Edited by Donald Gallup. New Haven: Ticknor & Fields, 1980. Poems written mainly when O'Neill was in his twenties.

Eugene O'Neill: The Unfinished Plays. Edited by Virginia Floyd. New York: Frederick Ungar, 1988. Contains notes and scenarios for three unwritten plays.

Eugene O'Neill: Work Diary, 1924–1943. Edited by Donald Gallup. 2 vols. New Haven: Yale University Library, 1981. A daily record of O'Neill's work habits. Important for dating the plays.

Long Day's Journey into Night. New Haven: Yale University Press, 1956. The original edition, frequently reprinted.

"Love and Admiration and Respect": The O'Neill-Commins Correspondence. Edited by Dorothy Commins. Durham: Duke University Press, 1986. Letters from O'Neill and his wife Carlotta Monterey to Saxe Commins, his editor and close friend. Includes Commins's reminiscence of the relationship.

Selected Bibliography

Selected Letters of Eugene O'Neill. Edited by Travis Bogard and Jackson Bryer. New Haven: Yale University Press, 1988. The most comprehensive, useful collection of O'Neill's correspondence; 560 letters spanning his life and career.

"The Theatre We Worked For": The Letters of Eugene O'Neill to Kenneth Macgowan. Edited by Jackson Bryer. New Haven: Yale University Press, 1982. Macgowan was O'Neill's theatrical producer and colleague. Informative.

The Unknown O'Neill: Unpublished or Unfamiliar Writings of Eugene O'Neill. Edited by Travis Bogard. New Haven: Yale University Press, 1988. A miscellany containing several stories and lesser known writings by O'Neill.

Secondary Works

Biography

Alexander, Doris. *The Tempering of Eugene O'Neill.* New York: Harcourt, Brace & World, 1962. Readable but not always reliable early biography. Covers O'Neill's formative years.

Boulton, Agnes. *Part of a Long Story.* New York: Doubleday, 1958. Fascinating account of O'Neill as a young artist, written by his second wife. Anecdotal.

Bowen, Croswell. *Curse of the Misbegotten: A Tale of the House of O'Neill.* New York: Ballantine Books, 1959. Supposedly written "with the assistance of Shane O'Neill," the playwright's son. Dubious.

Gelb, Arthur, and Barbara Gelb. *O'Neill.* Enlarged ed. New York: Harper and Row, 1973. The best single-volume biography.

Sheaffer, Louis. *O'Neill: Son and Playwright.* Boston: Little, Brown & Co., 1968. The first of two volumes; traces O'Neill's life through 1919.

———. *O'Neill: Son and Artist.* Boston: Little, Brown & Co., 1973. Takes O'Neill's life and career from 1920 to his death. This two-volume biography is the standard, most authoritative study of the playwright's life.

Critical Studies: Books

Barlow, Judith E. *Final Acts: The Creation of Three Late O'Neill Plays.* Athens: University of Georgia Press, 1985. Analyzes O'Neill's composition process. Includes a scholarly appraisal of his revisions for *Long Day's Journey into Night*.

Bentley, Eric. *Theatre of War: Modern Drama from Ibsen to Brecht.* New York: Viking Press, 1973. Contains a negative assessment of O'Neill's achievement, summing up Bentley's long-term hostility toward the playwright.

Berlin, Normand. *Eugene O'Neill.* New York: Grove Press, 1982. Readable, brief overview of O'Neill's career.

Bigsby, C. W. E. *A Critical Introduction to Twentieth-Century Drama, 1900–1940.* Vol. 1. Cambridge: Cambridge University Press, 1982. The section on O'Neill offers a shrewd, compact overview of his plays.

Bogard, Travis. *Contour in Time: The Plays of Eugene O'Neill.* New York: Oxford University Press, 1972; rev. 1988. The best-informed critical analysis of O'Neill's career. Combines historical, thematic, and biographical approaches.

Brustein, Robert. *The Theatre of Revolt.* Boston: Little, Brown & Co., 1964. An influential chapter surveys O'Neill's career, condemning the early plays as artistic failures but praising *Long Day's Journey into Night.*

Carpenter, Frederic I. *Eugene O'Neill.* Boston: Twayne Publishers, 1978. A concise discussion of the major plays.

Chabrowe, Leonard. *Ritual and Pathos: The Theater of O'Neill.* Lewisburg, Penn.: Bucknell University Press, 1976. Places O'Neill in the tradition of "religious" or "ritualistic" theater.

Chothia, Jean. *Forging a Language: A Study of the Plays of Eugene O'Neill.* Cambridge: Cambridge University Press, 1979. The first book-length discussion of O'Neill's use of language. Balanced and informative.

Clark, Barrett H. *Eugene O'Neill: The Man and His Plays.* New York: Dover, 1947. A revised edition of the first book-length study of O'Neill, one that was read by him. Still of interest for material on his early career.

Engel, Edwin. *The Haunted Heroes of Eugene O'Neill.* Cambridge, Mass.: Harvard University Press, 1953. An intelligent, occasionally sharp assessment of the first phase of O'Neill's career. Discusses Nietzsche, Jung, intellectual background.

Falk, Doris V. *Eugene O'Neill and the Tragic Tension.* New Brunswick: Rutgers University Press, 1958. A study of O'Neill's tragic form, heavily influenced by Jungian psychology.

Floyd, Virginia. *The Plays of Eugene O'Neill: A New Assessment.* New York: Frederick Ungar, 1985. A chronological survey of the plays, applying biographical criticism.

Manheim, Michael. *Eugene O'Neill's New Language of Kinship.* Syracuse, N.Y.: Syracuse University Press, 1982. Family relationships in the later plays. Includes lists of motifs for each character in *Long Day's Journey into Night.*

Selected Bibliography

Orlandello, John. *O'Neill on Film*. Madison, N.J.: Fairleigh Dickinson University Press, 1982. Contains an analysis of the film version of *Long Day's Journey into Night*.

Porter, Laurin. *The Banished Prince: Time, Memory, and Ritual in the Late Plays of Eugene O'Neill*. Ann Arbor, Mich.: UMI Research Press, 1988. The chapter on the play discusses how the four Tyrones seem trapped by time.

Raleigh, John Henry. *The Plays of Eugene O'Neill*. Carbondale: Southern Illinois University Press, 1965. Strong on cultural history; fine chapter on O'Neill as an American writer.

Ranald, Margaret Loftus. *The Eugene O'Neill Companion*. Westport, Conn.: Greenwood Press, 1984. Factual handbook on the playwright's life and works. Useful resource.

Robinson, James. *Eugene O'Neill and Oriental Thought: A Divided Vision*. Carbondale: Southern Illinois University Press, 1982. Absorbing discussion of the influence of Eastern philosophy and religion on O'Neill's thought.

Sarlos, Robert K. *Jig Cook and the Provincetown Players*. Amherst: University of Massachusetts Press, 1982. Contains the best view of O'Neill's association with the Provincetown Players at the launching of his career.

Sheibler, Rolf. *The Late Plays of Eugene O'Neill*. Bern: Francke Verlag, 1970. Contains a substantial analysis of *Long Day's Journey into Night*, with insights into Mary's character and the play's structure.

Tiusanen, Timo. *O'Neill's Scenic Images*. Princeton: Princeton University Press, 1968. Studies O'Neill's playwriting techniques with emphasis on nonverbal methods.

Törnqvist, Egil. *A Drama of Souls: Studies in O'Neill's Super-Naturalistic Technique*. New Haven: Yale University Press, 1969. A distinguished study, emphasizing O'Neill's technical innovations; includes discussion of O'Neill's tragic vision and theory of dramaturgy.

Wainscott, Ronald H. *Staging O'Neill: The Experimental Years, 1920–1934*. New Haven: Yale University Press, 1988. Detailed study of the production history of O'Neill's major plays (not including *Long Day's Journey into Night*).

Williams, Raymond. *Modern Tragedy*. Stanford: Stanford University Press, 1960. Analysis of modern tragedy from a Marxist perspective, with passing observations on O'Neill.

Winther, Sophus Keith. *Eugene O'Neill: A Critical Study*, 2d ed., enlarged. New York: Russell & Russell, 1961. Early evaluation of O'Neill's ideas, written by a personal friend.

Anthologies of Criticism

Bloom, Harold, ed. *Eugene O'Neill's "Long Day's Journey into Night."* New York: Chelsea House Publishers, 1987. A fine collection of commentaries on the play extracted from books by O'Neill's major critics.

Cargill, Oscar, N. Brillion Fagin, and William J. Fisher, eds. *O'Neill and His Plays: Four Decades of Criticism.* New York: New York University Press, 1961. A large collection of material, including statements by O'Neill and play reviews and articles by various critics.

Floyd, Virginia, ed. *Eugene O'Neill: A World View.* New York: Frederick Ungar, 1979. A collection of essays, mainly by foreign critics. Contains section on performances of *Long Day's Journey into Night.*

Gassner, John, ed. *O'Neill: A Collection of Critical Essays.* Englewood Cliffs, N.J.: Prentice-Hall, 1964. Reprints a variety of articles on O'Neill's work.

Griffen, Ernest G., ed. *Eugene O'Neill: A Collection of Criticism.* New York: McGraw-Hill Book Co., 1976. Includes a bibliography.

Martine, James, ed. *Critical Essays on Eugene O'Neill.* Boston: G. K. Hall & Co., 1984. A collection of original articles, including an extensive bibliographical essay as introduction.

Miller, Jordan Y. *Playwright's Progress: O'Neill and the Critics.* Chicago: Scott, Foresman & Co., 1965. A sampler of reviews of the plays.

Stroupe, John H., ed. *Critical Approaches to O'Neill.* New York: AMS Press, 1988. A collection of articles on various aspects of O'Neill's work, reprinted from *Comparative Drama.*

Journal Articles

Astington, John H. "Shakespeherian Rags." *Modern Drama* 31 (1988):72–80. Discusses the presence of Shakespeare in *Long Day's Journey into Night.*

Berlin, Normand. "Ghosts of the Past: O'Neill and Hamlet." *The Massachusetts Review* 20 (1979):312–23. Treats parallels between *Hamlet* and *Long Day's Journey into Night.*

Black, Stephen A. "Ella O'Neill's Addiction." *The Eugene O'Neill Newsletter* 9 (1985):24–26. Discusses how and why O'Neill's mother overcame her drug habit.

Einenkel, Robert. "Long Day's Journey Toward Separation: The Mary-Edmund Struggle." *The Eugene O'Neill Newsletter* 9 (1985):14–23. Analyzes Edmund's struggle to escape Mary's influence.

Hinden, Michael. "Missing Lines in *Long Day's Journey into Night.*" *Modern Drama,* 22 (1989):177–82. Announces the discovery of and analyzes several lines previously missing from the text.

Selected Bibliography

Mandl, Bette. "Wrestling with the Angel in the House: Mary Tyrone's Long Journey." *The Eugene O'Neill Newsletter* 12 (1988):19–23. Provides a feminist analysis of Mary's plight.

McDonald, David. "The Phenomenology of the Glance in *Long Day's Journey into Night.*" *Theatre Journal* 31 (1979):343–56. Theoretical analysis of nonverbal character interactions in the play.

Raleigh, John Henry. "O'Neill's *Long Day's Journey into Night* and New England Irish-Catholicism." *Partisan Review* 26 (1959):573–92. Suggests that the problems of the Tyrones are typical in some respects of New England Irish-Catholics.

Redford, Grant H. "Dramatic Art vs. Autobiography: A Look at *Long Day's Journey into Night.*" *College English* 25 (1964):527–35. Argues that the play is a controlled work of art, not merely a slice of life.

Rothenberg, Albert, and Eugene D. Shapiro. "The Defense of Psychoanalysis in Literature: *Long Day's Journey into Night* and *A View from the Bridge.*" *Comparative Drama* 7 (1973):51–67. Discusses structural tensions in the play based on the frequency of episodes of defensiveness in the family.

Rothenberg, Albert. "Autobiographical Drama: Strindberg and O'Neill." *Literature and Psychology* 17 (1967):95–114. Discusses O'Neill's attitude toward his mother as suggested by his plays.

Sheaffer, Louis. "Correcting Some Errors in Annals of O'Neill." *Comparative Drama* 17 (1983):201–32. Comments on issues in dispute among O'Neill's biographers.

Weismann, Philip. "Conscious and Unconscious Autobiographical Dramas of Eugene O'Neill." *Journal of the American Psychoanalytic Association* 5 (1957):432–60. A Freudian analysis of *Long Day's Journey into Night* and *Desire Under the Elms.*

Winther, Sophus Keith. "O'Neill's Tragic Themes: *Long Day's Journey into Night.*" *Arizona Quarterly* 13 (1957):295–307. Early appraisal.

Bibliography

Atkinson, Jennifer McCabe. *Eugene O'Neill: A Descriptive Bibliography.* Pittsburgh: University of Pittsburgh Press, 1974.

Miller, Jordan Y. *Eugene O'Neill and the American Critic: A Bibliographical Checklist,* 2d ed. rev. Hamden, Conn.: Archon Books, 1973. Summarizes reviews of productions and O'Neill's critical reception through 1972.

Reaver, J. Russell. *An O'Neill Concordance.* 3 vols. Detroit: Gale Research Co., 1969.

Sanborn, Ralph, and Barrett H. Clark. *A Bibliography of the Works of Eugene O'Neill.* New York: B. Blom, 1965.

Index

Index

Index

soliloquies. *See* monologues
sound effects, 25, 78
stage directions, 21–22, 41–42, 61
stammering, 5, 62–63, 65
Strindberg, August, 12
suicide attempts, 46–47, 52, 61–62, 105, 106, 107
Swedish Royal Dramatic Theatre, 10–11, 12
Swinburne, Algernon, 24, 73, 75
Symons, Arthur, 75

Tao House, 8
title (of play), 7, 31, 72, 79
Tolstoy, Leo: *Anna Karenina*, 17
Törnqvist, Egil, 41
tragic hero, 39, 81, 86–87
Tyrone, Edmund, discussed 60–67; mentioned on almost every page
Tyrone, Eugene, 26, 32, 39, 40, 43, 45, 54, 55, 56
Tyrone, James, discussed 47–52; mentioned on almost every page

Tyrone, James, Jr., discussed 53–60; mentioned on almost every page
Tyrone, Mary Cavan, discussed 39–47; mentioned on almost every page
Tyrone family, 6, 17, 23, 26, 27, 28, 33–36, 37–39, 45, 63–64, 67, 73, 97

visionary experience, 62–63, 67, 71, 72
Voltaire, François, 24

Walsh, Nettie, 103, 106
Whitman, Walt, 1, 24
Wilde, Oscar, 24, 75–76
Wilder, Thornton: *Our Town*, 6, 16
Williams, Tennessee, 91; *Glass Menagerie, The*, 6; *Streetcar Named Desire, A*, 16, 37
Wilson, August, 9; *Fences*, 6
Wilson, Lanford, 91

Zola, Émile, 24, 82–83, 85

About the Author

Michael Hinden is professor of English at the University of Wisconsin-Madison and chairman of the Board of Directors of the Eugene O'Neill Society. His publications include numerous essays on Eugene O'Neill, modern drama, and the theory of tragedy, as well as a collection of humorous verse. He has served as chairman of the Integrated Liberal Studies Program at the University of Wisconsin and is the recipient of a Distinguished Teaching Award. He also has served as Fulbright Senior Lecturer in American Literature at the University of Bucharest and as president of the Meiklejohn Education Foundation.